SAT®
POWER
VOCAB

2nd Edition

The Staff of The Princeton Review

PrincetonReview.com

WITHDRAWN

Penguin
Random
House

The Princeton Review
555 West 18th Street
New York, NY 10011
E-mail: editorialsupport@review.com

Published in the United States by Penguin
Random House LLC, New York, and in Canada
by Random House of Canada, a division of
Penguin Random House Ltd., Toronto.

Terms of Service: The Princeton Review Online
Companion Tools ("Student Tools") for retail
books are available for only the two most recent
editions of that book. Student Tools may be
activated only twice per eligible book purchased
for two consecutive 12-month periods, for a
total of 24 months of access. Activation of
Student Tools more than twice per book is in
direct violation of these Terms of Service and
may result in discontinuation of access to
Student Tools Services.

ISBN: 978-0-451-48754-4
eBook ISBN: 978-0-451-48755-1

The Princeton Review is not affiliated with
Princeton University.

Editor: Colleen Day
Production Editors: Kathy Carter and Liz Rutzel
Production Artist: Deborah A. Silvestrini

10 9 8 7 6 5 4 3 2 1

2nd Edition

Editorial

Rob Franek, Editor-in-Chief
Casey Cornelius, VP Content Development
Mary Beth Garrick, Director of Production
Selena Coppock, Managing Editor
Meave Shelton, Senior Editor
Colleen Day, Editor
Sarah Litt, Editor
Aaron Riccio, Editor
Orion McBean, Editorial Assistant

Penguin Random House Publishing Team

Tom Russell, VP, Publisher
Alison Stoltzfus, Publishing Director
Jake Eldred, Associate Managing Editor
Ellen Reed, Production Manager
Suzanne Lee, Designer

Acknowledgments

The Princeton Review would like to thank Jonathan Chiu and Gina Donegan for their fantastic work on this edition. Thanks also to everyone who contributed to the creation of this book: Debbie Silvestrini, Craig Patches, Kathy Carter, and Liz Rutzel.

Special thanks to Adam Robinson, who conceived of and perfected the Joe Bloggs approach to standardized tests and many of the other successful techniques used by The Princeton Review.

Contents

Register You

1 Go to **PrincetonReview.com/cracking**

2 You'll see a welcome page where you can register your book using the following ISBN: 9780451487544

3 After placing this free order, you'll either be asked to log in or to answer a few simple questions in order to set up a new Princeton Review account.

4 Finally, click on the "Student Tools" tab located at the top of the screen. It may take an hour or two for your registration to go through, but after that, you're good to go.

If you are experiencing book problems (potential content errors), please contact EditorialSupport@review.com with the full title of the book, its ISBN number (located above), and the page number of the error. Experiencing technical issues? Please e-mail TPRStudentTech@review.com with the following information:

- your full name
- e-mail address used to register the book
- full book title and ISBN
- your computer OS (Mac or PC) and Internet browser (Firefox, Safari, Chrome, etc.)
- description of technical issue

Book Online!

Once you've registered, you can...

- Find any late-breaking information released about the SAT

- Download and print the end-of-chapter word lists found in this book, as well as the Glossary of need-to-know terms

- Check out articles with valuable advice about college admissions

- Sort colleges by whatever you're looking for (such as Best Theater or Dorm), learn more about your top choices, and see how they all rank according to *The Best 381 Colleges*

- Check to see if there have been any corrections or updates to this edition

Offline Resources

- *Reading and Writing Workout for the SAT*

- *Word Smart*

- *More Word Smart*

The
Princeton
Review®

Introduction

Why You Need This Book

If you're reading this book, chances are you are preparing to take a major standardized test such as the SAT. Or perhaps you have already taken the SAT and will be taking it again in hopes of achieving a higher score. You may have heard that the SAT no longer tests vocabulary, but this is not entirely accurate. It is true that the SAT does not test *as much* vocabulary as it once did, but here at The Princeton Review we know that students with a strong vocabulary tend to get better scores. Why?

The College Board's SAT underwent a major change in March 2016. Prior to 2016, there were many questions (called Sentence Completions) that explicitly tested difficult vocabulary words. And if you go back further in time to when your parents took the test, for example, there were even more vocabulary-based questions, such as word analogies. In March 2016, Sentence Completions were removed from the SAT, and the entire Verbal portion of the exam was said to test only reading and grammar skills.

The dirty little secret about the SAT, however, is that you *still* need a strong knowledge of vocabulary in order to score well. Difficult words still appear in many Reading passages, questions, and answer choices, and if you don't know these words, you will probably struggle. The SAT contains at least 10–15 words that the average student may not know—which could be the difference between answering a question correctly and getting stuck.

At The Princeton Review, we know the SAT like the backs of our hands. We know what words you are likely to see on the SAT and which words you will not. More importantly, we know some effective strategies for learning unfamiliar vocabulary that do not require long hours spent memorizing endless lists of difficult words.

A Strong Vocabulary Is "Good for Your Brain"

You may be thinking, "There is more to life than a score on a standardized test." Yes, we agree. Although we eat, sleep, and breathe bubble sheets and #2 pencils, we do occasionally venture into the "real world." And, yes, you guessed it: Vocabulary is useful there, too.

The English language is impressive in its variety. Unabridged dictionaries can contain as many as 600,000 words, but if you count the myriad of technical words found in disciplines such as science, medicine, engineering, and law, there are likely about one million English words. None of us can learn all of these—nor do we need to—but the more words you know, the more you will understand the world around you. When a news anchor says that a bill has "bipartisan support" in Congress, you will be a more engaged citizen if you know what *bipartisan* means. (It means that both political parties support the legislation.)

A complaint we often hear from students is that the English language is *too* complex. For instance, why are there at least seven synonyms for *friendly* (*affable, amiable, amicable, amenable, cordial, genial, solicitous*, and so on) when we could all just say "friendly"? For the same reason there are there at least a million songs available to download when you could just listen to the same Beyoncé song all day. Variety is the spice of life!

Convinced yet? Well, what if we told you that having a stronger vocabulary can actually *make you smarter?* How can we make such a bold claim?

Psychology researchers Betty Hart and Todd Risley conducted an important study on preschoolers nearly 30 years ago. The study was simple: They counted the number of words that the preschoolers heard in their everyday lives from parents, siblings, playmates, television, and so on. They then tracked these children throughout the rest of their childhoods and measured how well they performed in school and, later, whether these children went to college, where they went to college, and what careers they pursued.

The results were startling and undeniable: The children who were exposed to the highest number of words were the most successful later in life. And here is the best part: It was not only the *quantity* of words they were exposed to, but also the *diversity* of words that affected the final outcome. In short, knowing seven different words for *friendly* is not just a strategy to boost your Scrabble game; it might actually *make you smarter*.

Scientific evidence that vocabulary is "good for your brain" is a good motivation for learning some. This book will show you the way.

Who Needs This Book?

Some might tell you that the best and easiest way to learn vocabulary is to learn it naturally over the course of a lifetime: from your friends, parents, teachers, the media, books, and so on. After all, that's how you first learned many of the words you use every day.

While there is no substitute for the natural, organic way of learning vocabulary from reading and real-life interactions, if you feel that your vocabulary is weaker than it should be, you need a *fast* way to bring yourself up to speed. Reading the world's great classic works of literature and listening to hours of NPR on the car radio takes *years* of dedication. There *is* a faster way.

This book is written for people at all levels of English knowledge and expertise. Maybe you are relatively new to the English language, know the basics, and now want to learn more challenging words. This book is for you. Maybe you are a native speaker and want to expand upon what you already know. This book is for you. Most of you probably have an average vocabulary. This book is for everyone. We guarantee that you will learn a lot of new words, and that you will see many of these words when you take the SAT.

How to Use This Book

SAT Power Vocab is designed to let you learn vocabulary in a logical manner, gradually, and with strategies and practice to ensure that you will remember new words for more than just a few minutes. For the best results, we recommend you read the chapters in this book in order and in their entirety, as each chapter builds on the one before it. The chapters are fairly short, so you can read them anytime, anywhere: during study hall, on a bus trip, or before bed. You can use this book over a long period of time or read it all in the week or two before your exam. Cramming is not the ideal way to learn anything, but it's better than not studying at all.

Tricks of the Trade

The most common question we get from students is this: *How* do I learn vocabulary? Well, different approaches work for different people, but we at The Princeton Review believe in a multilayered approach that incorporates etymology (word roots), mnemonics, and more—plus practice exercises and activities to hone your word skills.

Word Roots

In Chapters 1 through 4, we will explore the fundamental building blocks of words. English is, in fact, cobbled together from other languages, including Latin and Greek. Many English words contain roots with meanings derived from those languages. When you learn some common roots, you will find that you can decipher the meaning of a word on sight even if you've never seen or heard it before.

For example, let's look at the Greek root *chron-*, which relates to time. The words below contain the root *chron-* and all have to do with time in some way.

---

chronological: in order according to time

syn**chron**ize: to put on the same timetable

ana**chron**ism: something out of place in time or history

chronic: continuing over a long time

chronicle: chronological record of events

chronometer: device to measure time

The Advantages of Learning Etymology

Learning word roots is a key part of etymology, which is the study of the origin of words and how their meanings have changed over time. The principal advantages of using etymology to remember a definition are: (1) A word's etymology tells you something about the meaning of the word, and (2) the same etymology may be shared by lots of words, which, in turn, can help you remember the meanings of clusters of related words. Moreover, learning etymology can get you interested in the origin of words and language in general; etymology tells you a story of a word through the centuries.

The Pitfalls of Learning Etymology

Most of the time, etymology helps you to decipher the meanings of words. In rare cases, however, it can lead you astray. The etymology of a word will usually tell you *something* about the meaning, but it will rarely gives you the full definition. Students often confuse a word's etymology with its meaning, which can lead to errors on the SAT.

For example, on a certain SAT, many students got a question wrong because they thought that the word *verdant* was etymologically related to words like *verify, verdict, verisimilitude,* and *veritable. Verdant* must have something to do with the concept of truth or reality, they reasoned.

This is clever thinking, but it's wrong. *Verdant* comes from a different family of words with the same root as the French word *vert,* which means "green." If those same students had recognized that connection, they might have realized that *verdant* means "green with vegetation," as in *a verdant forest.*

Similarly, a lot of words that begin with *ped-* have something to do with feet: *pedestrian, pedal, pedestal, pedometer, impede, expedite.* A *pediatrician,* however, is *not* a foot doctor. A *pediatrician* is a doctor for children. A *podiatrist* is a foot doctor. (The word *pediatrician* is, however, related to the word meaning a strict teacher of children: *pedagogue.*)

Despite these sorts of exceptions, etymology is a powerful tool to remember words that you already know and to successfully determine the meanings of words you don't know.

Mnemonics

A mnemonic (pronounced "ni-MON-ick") is a device or trick that helps you remember something specific. Grade-schoolers are sometimes taught to remember the spelling of *arithmetic* by using the following mnemonic: **A R**at **I**n **T**he **H**ouse **M**ight **E**at **T**om's **I**ce **C**ream. The first letter in each word in this silly sentence stands for the letters in *arithmetic.* Remember the sentence and you remember how to spell the word. Mnemonics can appeal to our ears, too. Take this popular history mnemonic: *In fourteen hundred ninety-two, Columbus sailed the ocean blue.* Or this spelling mnemonic: *"i" before "e" except after "c," and in words that say "a," as in "neighbor" and "weigh"*?

Some vocabulary words do not have obvious roots, or their meanings are still fuzzy even when you notice the roots. For these stubborn characters, we can use mnemonics to remember even the strangest members of the English language. In Chapter 5, we provide a bunch of suggested mnemonics, but you may have fun creating your own as well in Chapter 6.

Word associations are also types of mnemonics. For example, the word *alleviate* might remind you of the name of a popular over-the-counter pain reliever. That's right: To *alleviate* is to relieve pain. Associating a word with an idea, phrase, object that is related in meaning can help you remember the actual definition of the word. We take a closer look at this strategy (and provide lots of practice) in Chapter 7.

Practice and Puzzles

Even with roots and mnemonics at your disposal, practice is no doubt the key to learning—and remembering—challenging words. Using flashcards and similar study tactics are definitely useful (we discuss flashcards later in this book), but practice is often more effective (and interesting) when there is a task to complete. In this book, you'll find exercises that test your knowledge of word relationships, synonyms, and roots, as well as how to determine the meaning of words in context. Starting in Chapter 6, there are also a bunch of SAT "quick quizzes," which give you first-hand experience with the kind of vocabulary-in-context questions you will see on the SAT. For the best results, do all of the practice exercises at the end of a chapter before you move on to the next one.

Math Vocabulary

The bulk of this book is dedicated to helping you succeed on the verbal portion of the SAT, especially the Reading section, where you'll likely encounter the most vocabulary words. However, discussions about vocabulary often leave out math terms, which are just as essential to your success on the SAT. In order to do well on the Math Test, you need to know what the questions are asking you—and that all begins with understanding key math terms. Chapter 10 serves as a glossary of the most important math vocabulary you should know for the exam. If you need to brush up on the definitions of *integer* or *coefficient*, for instance, this chapter will guide the way.

Strategies, Word Lists, and More

Last but not least, the Conclusion provides tips for taking your vocab prep beyond this book. Our step-by-step approach for learning and remembering key vocabulary will help you on the SAT, in the classroom or workplace, and in your daily life.

You can start with the words in this book, which are compiled in end-of-chapter word lists throughout the book as well as a comprehensive Glossary on page 305. (The Glossary also provides a "Cram List" of the 50 most important words to know for the SAT.) Both the end-of-chapter word lists and Glossary can also be found online in your Student Tools. (See Register Your Book Online! on page vi to access these resources.) Feel free to print these out so that they can serve as study guides on the go, or use them to make flashcards. How you study is up to you.

Two Final Words of Advice: Be Suspicious

You already know some of the words in the book. You may know quite a few of them. Naturally, you don't need to drill yourself on words you already know and use.

But be careful. Before skipping a word, be sure that you really do know what it means. Some of the most embarrassing vocabulary mistakes occur when a person confidently uses familiar words incorrectly.

Now it's time to start learning some vocabulary! But before you dive in to Chapter 1, take a little bit of time to study our pronunciation key on the following page.

Pronunciation Key

The pronunciations you will find in this book differ slightly from the pronunciation keys found in most dictionaries. Our key is based on consistent phonetic sounds, so you don't have to memorize it. All consonants not found in this table are pronounced as you would expect. Capitalized letters are accented.

The Letter(s)	Is (Are) Pronounced Like the Letter(s)	In the Word(s)
a	a	bat, can
ah	o	con, bond
aw	aw	paw, straw
ay	a	skate, rake
e	e	stem, hem
ee	ea	steam, clean
i	i	rim, chin, hint
ing	ing	sing, ring
oh	o	row, tow
oo	oo	room, boom
ow	ow	cow, brow
oy	oy	boy, toy
u, uh	u	run, bun
y (ye, eye)	i	climb, time
ch	ch	chair, chin
f	f, ph	film, phony
g	g	go, goon
j	j	join, jungle
k	c	cool, cat

s	s	solid, wisp
sh	sh	shoe, wish
z	z	zoo, razor
zh	s	measure
uh	a	apologize

Etymology

PART 1

Etymology

Basic Word Roots

Get Back to Your Roots

The traditional and perhaps tedious way to learn vocabulary is memorizing hundreds of words, drilling them into your brain over and over again until your head spins. However, this is not the approach we take in this book. (Remember, studying vocabulary for the SAT no longer requires rote memorization.) A far more productive way to prepare for the exam, and one of the strategies we will focus on in this book, is to learn the building blocks of many English words and use those building blocks to figure out the meanings of words that challenge you. Not all English words contain common word roots, but many of the most challenging ones do, including many found on the SAT.

For example, one of the longest, most notorious words in the English language is

antidisestablishmentarianism

This word may look ridiculous, and we promise you will never see it on a standardized test. But it's a good example of how roots can help you. Break the word up like this:

anti + *dis* + *establishment* + *arian* + *ism*

Now try to figure out the meaning. *Anti-* and *dis-* are both negative roots, and two negatives can cancel each other out and become a positive. We all know what *establishment* is: an organized, preset way of doing something. An *-arian* is a person (think *vegetarian*). An *-ism* is a belief. So this word must refer to people who share a belief in keeping the established order, or an idea shared by people opposed to change.

Actually, *antidisestablishmentarianism* is a little more specific than that. It pertains to the movement to keep the government's "established" support of the church intact in 19th-century England. Still, as shown in this example, knowledge of word roots can get you very close to this meaning—without having to open a dictionary!

We promise you won't see any words in this book nearly as long as the one above. But many words involve similar building blocks, so in this chapter we'll look at some of the most common ones. Some of them may be new to you, and some of them you may already know. Let's get

started! To keep you organized, we will present them in alphabetical order.

a- without; not

Put *a-* in front of a common word and it usually indicates that something is *not* true.

- If you are **apolitical,** then you are *not* a political person.

- If you are **amoral,** then you are *not* concerned with the morality of a situation.

Don't get too carried away with *a-*, though. This prefix works only if it is placed in front of another root. (An apple is not a fruit that is without *pple,* for example.)

an-, ana- against

Just like *a-*, the prefixes *an-* and *ana-* usually indicate a negative relationship within the word.

- **Anaerobic** exercise means "without air."

- An **anagram** is a word whose letters have been scrambled, i.e., *against* the usual order.

anti-   against; opposite

This is yet another negative prefix. The possibilities are endless:

- If you are **antiauthority**, you are *opposed* to authority figures.

- An **anticancer** drug fights cancer, while an **antidepressant** helps to combat (oppose) depression.

- In late 18th-century America, an **Anti-Federalist** was *opposed* to excessive federal power.

You get the idea. (Please note that *anti-* is not the same as *ante-*, which means "before.")

auto-   self

Why is it called an **automatic** dishwasher? Because it washes dishes by it*self* (after you load the machine, of course).

- How did the **automobile** get its name? A hundred years ago, it was remarkable to see a vehicle that moved by *itself* (as opposed to a horse-drawn cart).

- Your **autograph** is your own *self*'s unique handwriting.

- An **autobiography** is a biography that you write about *yourself*.

co-, con-   with; together

Co- at the beginning of a word means "with" or "together."

- **Coauthors** collaborate on a book *together*.

- **Coworkers** work *together*.

contra-   against

- When you **contradict** someone, you say something *against* his or her point of view.

- A **contrary** opinion is one not in agreement with (or that goes *against*) the majority.

- **Controversy** occurs when two or more people disagree.

de-   **reduce; remove**
- When you **deduct** money from your bank account, you *remove* it.

- **Deceleration** is the opposite of acceleration. You are *reducing* your speed.

- To **dethrone** a king is to *remove* him from the throne.

- When you **debug** your computer, you *remove* the "bugs," i.e., viruses or glitches.

ex-   **out**
- The **exterior** of your house is the *outer* portion.

- To **exhale** is to breathe *out*.

- Archaeologists **excavate** a site by digging *out* the dirt that surrounds an artifact.

- The **ex**-Congressman left, or came *out*, of Congress. He is no longer in office.

im-, in-   **not; without**

Lots of words start with *im-* and *in-*, and they are almost all negative in meaning.
- **Impossible** means "not possible."

- **Inappropriate** means "not appropriate."

magna-   **great; large**
- To call something **magnificent** suggests that it is a *great* achievement.

- To **magnify** is to make something *larger*.

- A **magnate** is a *great* or powerful person, especially in business.

mis-   bad; wrong; hate

Mis- is another negative prefix.

- When your little brother **misbehaves**, he behaves *badly*.
- If a book contains a **misprint**, the words were printed in the *wrong* way.

morph-   shape

When things **morph**, they change *shape*. *Morph-* can also be combined with other roots to form new words.

- **Metamorphosis** occurs when a caterpillar turns into a butterfly. It changes *shape*.

Q: Go back to the prefix *a-*. What does *amorphous* mean? (Turn to page 10 for the answer.)

---

non-   not; without

English is full of negative roots. *Non-* is yet another of these pessimistic characters.

- **Nonsense** is an idea that does *not* make any sense.
- **Nonfiction** is a type of writing that does *not* contain any fictional elements; it is real.
- Something that is **nondescript** has no real description; it is difficult to describe.

omni-   all

- **Omnivorous** animals are not simply carnivorous (eating meat) or herbivorous (eating animals); they eat *all* foods.
- **Omniscience** is the ability to "know *all*." (*Science* is the pursuit of knowledge.)
- **Omnipotence** is the quality of being *all*-powerful. (*Potency* is power.)
- **Omnipresence** is the quality of being present everywhere, in *all* places.

peri- around

- Finding the **perimeter** of a rectangle means finding the complete distance *around* the shape.

- Having **peripheral** vision gives you the ability to see *around* your normal line of sight.

post- after

- To **postpone** an activity is to plan to complete it *after* its originally targeted deadline.

- The **post-game** show happens *after* the football game has ended.

- A **postmortem** is a medical examination of a body *after* its death. (What is *mort-*? You guessed it: death.)

pre- before

- To **prepare** is to get ready for something *before* it happens.

- A **prediction** is a statement about the future *before* it happens.

- The Constitutional **Preamble** is the beginning of America's founding document. It comes *before* the Bill of Rights.

re- again

- If your teacher tells you to **redo** your homework, you need to do it *again*.

- When you **refresh** the page in your web browser, the page loads *again.*

- A **rebound** in basketball allows the player to grab the ball *again*, after it bounces off the backboard.

sub- under

- The city **subway** runs *under* the streets and buildings above (literally, "under the way").

- A **submarine** travels *under* the surface of the ocean. (*Marine* means "relating to the sea or ocean.")

- If your schoolwork is **substandard**, it is *below* the usual standards of excellence.

super- higher; better

- **Superman**, with his X-ray vision and **superhuman** strength is above ("higher than") that of mere mortals.

- The **Super Bowl** is the best and most competitive football game of the season.

- **Supersonic** airplanes can travel faster than the speed of sound. (*Son-* means "sound.")

A: *Amorphous* means "having no shape."

trans- across

- To **transfer** is to move *across* something.

- The **Transcontinental** Railroad of the 19th century allowed passengers to travel *across* the entire continent on a train.

- To **transmit** sound is to move it from one place to another.

Got all of that? Great! Now it's time to put your newfound knowledge to the test by completing the exercises on the next page.

Chapter 1 Practice Exercises

Synonyms

Using your knowledge of word roots, match the word on the left with the word most similar in meaning on the right. Answers can be found on page 16.

Set 1

1. antiauthority	a. change
2. automatic	b. collaborate
3. coauthor (v.)	c. hollow
4. contrary	d. increase
5. decelerate	e. involuntary
6. excavate	f. opposed
7. magnificent	g. rebellious
8. magnify	h. slow
9. morph	i. splendid
10. metamorphosis	j. transformation

Set 2

1. nonfiction	a. all-knowing
2. nonsense	b. all-powerful
3. nondescript	c. defer
4. omniscient	d. everywhere
5. omnipotent	e. external
6. omnipresent	f. foolishness
7. peripheral	g. indistinct
8. postpone	h. prophecy
9. prediction	i. recover
10. rebound	j. unimagined

Words in Context

Read each passage and determine the meaning of the words in bold based on the context of the paragraph. Answers can be found on page 16.

Most of the tomatoes I found at the supermarket had been shipped in from Canada, where they had been grown hydroponically in greenhouses. These were salad-sized "beefsteak" tomatoes, each one more perfectly round than the last, and basically **indistinguishable** in appearance from a large, deep pink racquetball.

1. **indistinguishable**_____

_____

2. **to distinguish**_____

_____

In 1752, Benjamin Franklin demonstrated through a series of kite experiments that lightning is a form of electricity. More than 250 years later, scientists still know relatively little about the causes of this **phenomenon**. Yet lightning plays such a significant role in weather and climate that it could eventually become a powerful tool in storm prediction. Current technology can detect the direction of a storm's wind flow but cannot tell if these winds will pick up or die down. Lightning commonly occurs during tornadoes, and flashes increase significantly right before a twister touches ground. If understood, lightning, once considered a mysterious and frightening occurrence, could do much to save lives.

3. **phenomenon** _____

_____

People often base their perceptions of similarity between fraternal twins on factors other than actual physical resemblance. Mannerisms such as similar gestures and facial expressions can substantially amplify even a minor resemblance. Fraternal twins, who are no closer genetically than ordinary siblings, are very likely to share many of these behavioral **quirks**, since they often spend more time together than do siblings with a separation in age. Consequently, because they constantly provide each other with nonverbal feedback, they tend to converge in many of their unconscious habits, leading to a closer perceived resemblance to one another.

4. **quirk** _____

_____

Bonus Word Roots

Study the definition of the words below and answer the questions that follow. Answers can be found on page 17.

- **CIRCUMNAVIGATE** (sur kum NAV uh gayt) *v*   to sail or travel all the way around

- **CIRCUMSCRIBE** (SUR kum skrybe) *v*   to draw a line around; to set the limits; to define; to restrict

- **CIRCUMVENT** (sur kum VENT) *v*   to get around something in a clever, occasionally dishonest way

1. What does it mean to **navigate**? _____

    _____

2. What is a **scribe**? _____

    _____

3. What does a **vent** do? _____

    _____

4. What is a circle's **circumference**?_____

    _____

5. What does the root *circum-* mean? _____

    _____

Questions 6–9: Read the following passage, paying attention to the words in bold, and answer the questions that follow.

Why do we know so little about the life of William Shakespeare when we know comparatively so much about the lives of his less accomplished peers? Our lack of knowledge about Shakespeare has inspired countless conspiracy theories. The actual writing of Shakespeare's works has been attributed to others from contemporary playwrights Christopher Marlowe and Ben Johnson to the brilliant Renaissance scientist and philosopher Francis Bacon. Shakespeare was an immensely successful dramatist as well as a prosperous property owner. **Circumspect**, and only too aware of the government-inspired branding of Johnson, its torture of Thomas Kyd, and its murder of Marlowe, Shakespeare kept himself nearly anonymous. **Wary** to the end, Shakespeare led a life virtually without memorable incident, as far as we can tell.

6. **Circumspect** and **wary** are synonyms. In the context of the passage, what do they mean? _____

_____

7. Write down three words that start with *spect-:*

_____

_____

_____

8. What does the root *spect-* relate to? _____

_____

9. How do the roots *circum-* and *spect-* relate to the definition of **circumspect**? _____

_____

Chapter 1 Answer Key

Synonyms

Set 1	Set 2
1. g	1. j
2. e	2. f
3. b	3. g
4. f	4. a
5. h	5. b
6. c	6. d
7. i	7. e
8. d	8. c
9. a	9. h
10. j	10. i

Words in Context

1. Since the tomatoes are perfectly round, they are similar or virtually identical to a racquetball, making them **indistinguishable**, which means "difficult to understand or make out."
2. Since one cannot see or notice the difference between a tomato and a racquetball, to **distinguish** must mean "to see or notice differences."
3. The entire passage is about lightning, a scientific occurrence studied by Benjamin Franklin and others. A **phenomenon** is simply an observable event, though the word is often used to describe something unusual.
4. The best clues here are "mannerisms" and "unconscious habits." **Quirks** are unusual characteristics in a person or idea.

Bonus Word Roots

1. To **navigate** means to travel over a planned course.
2. A **scribe** is a writer.
3. A **vent** is an opening that permits the escape of something.
4. The **circumference** of a circle is its perimeter.
5. The root *circum-* means "around."
6. In the passage, **circumspect** and **wary** mean "cautious." "Branding," "torture," and "murder" are all scary prospects, so Shakespeare would have been cautious and careful (demonstrated by the fact that he kept himself anonymous).
7. **spectator, spectacle, inspect** (There are others; these are just suggestions!)
8. The root *spect-* relates to looking or watching.
9. **Circumspect** literally means "looking around" (cautiously), which combines the roots *circum-* and *spect-*.

Chapter 1 Word List

Here is an alphabetical list of the most important words you learned in this chapter.

AMORAL (ay MOR ul) *adj* lacking a sense of right and wrong; neither good nor bad, neither moral nor immoral; without moral feelings
* Very young children are *amoral;* when they cry, they aren't being bad or good—they're merely doing what they have to do.

AMORPHOUS (uh MOR fus) *adj* shapeless; without a regular or stable shape; blob-like
* The sleepy little town was engulfed by an *amorphous* blob of glowing protoplasm—a higher intelligence from outer space.
* To say that something has an "*amorphous* shape" is a contradiction. How can a shape be shapeless?

CIRCUMNAVIGATE (sur kum NAV uh gayt) *v* to sail or travel all the way around
* Magellan's crew was the first to *circumnavigate* the globe.
* *Circumnavigating* their block took the little boys most of the morning because they stopped in nearly every yard to play with their new action figures.

The word can also be used figuratively.
* Jefferson skillfully *circumnavigated* the subject of his retirement; in his hour-long speech, he talked about everything but it.

CIRCUMSCRIBE (SUR kum skrybe) *v* to draw a line around; to set the limits; to define; to restrict
* The Constitution clearly *circumscribes* the restrictions that can be placed on our personal freedoms.
* A barbed-wire fence and armed guards *circumscribed* the movement of the prisoners.

CIRCUMSPECT (SUR kum spekt) *adj*   cautious
- As a public speaker, Nick was extremely *circumspect;* he always took great care not to say the wrong thing or give offense.
- The *circumspect* general did everything he could to keep his soldiers from unnecessary risk.

The word *circumspect* comes from Greek roots meaning "around" and "look" (as do the words *circle* and *inspect*). To be *circumspect* is to look around carefully before doing something.

CIRCUMVENT (sur kum VENT) *v* to get around something in a clever, occasionally dishonest way
- Our hopes for an early end of the meeting were *circumvented* by the chairperson's refusal to deal with the items on the agenda.
- The angry school board *circumvented* the students' effort to install televisions in every classroom.

DISTINGUISH (di STING gwish) *v*   to tell apart; to cause to stand out
- The rodent expert's eyesight was so acute that he was able to *distinguish* between a shrew and a vole from more than 500 feet away.
- I studied and studied but I was never able to *distinguish* between *discrete* and *discreet*.
- His face had no *distinguishing* characteristics; there was nothing about his features that stuck in your memory.
- Lou's uneventful career as a dogcatcher was not *distinguished* by adventure or excitement.

MAGNATE (MAG nayt) *n* a rich, powerful, or very successful businessperson
- After graduating from Harvard Business School, she became a *magnate* in the music industry, owning several record labels and production companies.

METAMORPHOSIS (met uh MOR fuh sis) *n* a magical change in form; a striking or sudden change

- Damon's *metamorphosis* from college student to Hollywood superstar was so sudden that it seemed a bit unreal.

The verb is *metamorphose*. To undergo a *metamorphosis* is to *metamorphose.*

OMNISCIENT (ahm NISH unt) *adj* all-knowing; having infinite wisdom
Omni- is a prefix meaning "all."

- To be *omnipotent* (ahm NIP uh tunt) is to be all-powerful.

- An *omnivorous* (ahm NIV ur us) animal eats all kinds of food, including meat and plants.

- Something *omnipresent* (AHM ni prez unt) seems to be every-where. In March, mud is *omnipresent.*

- The novel's narrator has an *omniscient* point of view, so his words often clue the reader in to things the characters in the story don't know. (Note: *Sci-* is a root meaning "knowledge" or "knowing." *Prescient* (PRESH unt) means knowing before-hand; *nescient* (NESH unt) means not knowing, or ignorant.)

PERIPHERY (puh RIF uh ree) *n* the outside edge of something

- José never got involved in any of our activities; he was always at the *periphery.*

- The professional finger painter enjoyed his position at the *periphery* of the art world.

To be at the *periphery* is to be *peripheral* (puh RIF uh rul). A *peripheral* interest, for example, is a secondary or side interest.

CHAPTER 2

Latin Roots and Feeling Words

Chapter 1 Review

Before beginning Chapter 2, let's see how much you remember from the previous chapter with this fill-in-the-blank exercise. You can check your answers on page 36.

1. A moral person does right; an immoral person does wrong; an **amoral** person _____.

2. Ed's art teacher said that his sculpture was **amorphous**; it was _____.

3. John D. Rockefeller was a **magnate**. *Magna*- means _____, so a magnate is a _____ person.

4. Every night, Dr. Jekyll underwent a bizarre **metamorphosis**: He _____ into Mr. Hyde.

5. When Lucy was a small child, she thought her parents were **omniscient**. Now that she's a teenager, she realizes that they don't _____.

6. Your **peripheral** vision is your ability to see _____.

Latin is Not a Dead Language

As mentioned earlier, many of the most challenging words in the English language derive their sounds and meanings from Latin. Don't worry; you need not memorize any complex conjugations in order to understand a few basic Latin roots. And we promise that knowing these roots will make learning multiple words a whole lot easier.

What Are "Feeling Words"?

Test writers love to test you on "feeling words," which usually appear on the Reading section of the SAT. A feeling word is exactly what it sounds like—a word that describes an emotion or state of being. Whenever a question asks about the author's tone or the attitude of a particular character, feeling words usually come into play. You know the basic emotions: happy, sad, angry, fearful, and so on. But on a standardized test you are more likely to see higher-level vocabulary words like *jubilant, despondent, indignant*, or *apprehensive* to describe emotions. Take a look at the following example:

> In line 20, the author mentions "jelly beans" in order to demonstrate that he is
>
> A) jubilant at the sight of a familiar treat.
>
> B) despondent at the end of each school day.
>
> C) indignant at the sight of more food.
>
> D) apprehensive at mealtimes.

These words *do* mean "happy" (jubilant), "sad" (despondent), "angry" (indignant), and "fearful" (apprehensive).

Why is the English language so complex? Don't ask why; let's just roll up our sleeves and learn some feeling words!

The list that follows contains some common Latin roots that show up in many words, including feeling words you should be familiar with, particularly for the SAT. Consider making flashcards for this list, with the root on the front of the card and various words the root appears in on the back.

Feeling Words with Latin Roots

vol- to wish; to will; to want

Let's start with a word we all know: volunteer. A **volunteer** is someone who acts upon his or her own desires or **volition**. A volunteer is not forced and does not require money to motivate his or her actions.

So, words with *vol-* inevitably involve wishes and desires, otherwise known as feelings. Keep reading to see examples of *vol-* combined with other roots to form some common test words, such as *benevolent, malevolent,* and others.

bene- kindness; goodness

Words you know that start with *bene-* are always good. (This lesson will **benefit** you. It will be **beneficial**.)

So, what does it mean if you are **benevolent**? You guessed it: You have kind wishes toward others.

Here are some other *bene-* words:

> **benediction** (n.)—an expression of kindness; a blessing
>
> **benefactor** (n.)—one who performs an act of kindness
>
> **beneficent** (adj.)—performing acts of charity
>
> **beneficiary** (n.)—one who receives a benefit
>
> **benign** (adj.)—kind and gentle

mal-   bad; ill; wrong

If you recall the villain **Maleficent** from the animated version of *Sleeping Beauty* (or the more recent Angelina Jolie film), this root will be an easy enough one to remember. *Maleficent* is not just a nasty-sounding name; it is an adjective used to describe anyone who is harmful or **malicious** in intent.

In medicine, what do doctors mean when they call a tumor *benign*? They don't mean the tumor is nice and gentle; rather, a benign tumor is simply "not harmful."

Q: What do doctors call a harmful tumor? See page 27 for the answer!

Let's go back to our good friend *vol-*. If **benevolent** means having kind wishes toward others, then what does **malevolent** mean? Yes, you're right: having *bad* wishes toward others.

Here are some other *mal-* words:

> **maladapted** (adj.)—not adapted well to the environment
>
> **malaise** (n.)—a general sense of unease
>
> **malcontent** (adj.)—dissatisfied (not content); (n.)—a person who is not content
>
> **malfeasance** (n.)—misconduct
>
> **malice** (n.)—a desire to harm others
>
> **malpractice** (n.)—harmful actions, especially by a doctor or lawyer

ambi-   both; changing

Ever wish you were **ambidextrous**? You probably know that this word refers to someone who is equally skilled with both hands. So, *ambi-* means "both" or "the ability to change." (And **dexterous** means "skillful with one's hands." We can tell you're getting the hang of this!)

Sounds Like: "Before Thought"

In legal jargon, "**malice** aforethought" means the commission of a crime with a premeditated intention of causing harm. (It also sounds like a line from Shakespeare, but it's not.)

What does it mean to be **ambivalent**? To have two or more conflicting emotions. If you have sharp eyes, you may have noticed that that's *val-*, not *vol-*. Not to worry. Sometimes the spellings of roots can change, but the meaning is still the same.

Another important *ambi-* word you absolutely need to know is **ambiguous:**

- When her mother asked her if she had completed her homework, Emily gave an *ambiguous* reply.

- Even after a thorough police investigation, the identity of the shoplifter remained *ambiguous*.

Based on these contexts, we can define **ambiguous** as unclear in meaning, confusing, or capable of being interpreted in different ways.

equi- equal; *voc-* speaking

While we're on the subject of vagueness, let's look at a word that means almost the same thing: **equivocal**.

Equivocal is made up of two important roots: *equi-* and *voc-*. You have seen both of these roots before in

A: A harmful tumor is known as a **malignant** tumor.

simple words such as **equal** and **vocal**. So, literally, being **equivocal** means "saying two things equally." In other words, you're being *ambiguous* with the intention of misleading others, or you're being hesitant about making a commitment.

- The politician would often *equivocate* when asked about a controversial issue.

- Samantha told James *unequivocally* that she would never go to the prom with him.

Equi- (or *equa-*) and *voc-* can be found in a number of English words. Here are a few important ones to remember:

advocate (n.)—a person who argues in favor of a position or cause; (v.)—to argue in favor of a position or cause

equanimity (n.)—staying calm and even-tempered (an "equal" mood)

equation (n.)—a statement asserting the equality of two expressions

equidistant (adj.)—equally distant

equilateral (adj.)—sharing equal sides

equitable (adj.)—fair and just ("equally" treated)

evoke (v.)—to call forth

invoke (v.)—to call upon a higher power

irrevocable (adj.)—something that cannot be stopped (or "called" back)

provoke (v.)—to cause, especially by speaking words (The adjective is *provocative*, which means "causing discussion, thought, emotion, or excitement in some way.")

vociferate (v.)—to speak loudly

vociferous (adj.)—talking a lot or loudly

plac- to calm or please

Ever hear of Lake **Placid** in the state of New York? How about a **placebo** medicine? You may be wondering what in the world these things have in common. Well, they both start with *plac-*, our next important root. Lake Placid is calm and gentle, and a placebo medicine may make you feel calm and healed, though it actually provides no medicinal value. Here are some other important *plac-* words:

Horse Whisperer?

Sometimes words look like they contain a certain root word, but, in fact, do not. Take the word *equine*, for example. It appears to start with *equi-*, but it is actually derived from a different Latin root, *equus*, which pertains to horses. But don't worry. At least 90% of the time, your knowledge of roots will *not* steer you wrong.

complacent (adj.)—satisfied with the current situation and uninterested in change

complaisant (adj.)—having a desire to please others

implacable (adj.)—impossible to calm or soothe

placate (v.)—to calm or soothe

We've learned a lot of words and word roots so far. Do you need to memorize them all? *Mal*arkey! If you remember the roots from this chapter and Chapter 1 (as well as those to come in future chapters) you'll be able to quickly decipher the general meaning of tons of words.

Complacent vs. *Complaisant*

Complacent and *complaisant* are obviously visually similar and are pronounced identically. As you can see, however, they have slightly different meanings. (English is cruel!) Test writers are far more likely to test you on *complacent*, so remember this when you're studying!

Chapter 2 Practice Exercises

Fill in the Blank

Fill in the blank with the word from this chapter that best completes the meaning of the sentence. Answers can be found on page 36.

1. Lake _____ derives its name from its smooth, glassy surface and the soothing mountain air in its environment.

2. A _____ person wishes harm on others.

3. Since Robert was an only child, he was the sole _____ to his father's estate.

4. You should not take action based on the wishes of others. Act on your own _____.

5. The crying baby was _____; no amount of rocking could console her.

6. Alex was a passionate _____ for the rights of animals.

7. If three sides of a triangle are equal, the triangle is _____.

8. Since their teacher was so _____, the students could rarely get a word in edgewise.

9. Many minority groups in America have fought to achieve rights _____ to that of the majority population.

10. The unqualified lawyer was often sued for _____.

Multiple Choice

Read each question and choose the best answer of the options given. Answers can be found on page 36.

Question 1 is based on the passage below.

> The doctor packed his instruments and left Keswick manor, stepping into the cool grey of a London morning. As he passed Whitehouse Street, his lip curled and his pace quickened. Here were the shabby offices of his nominal
> 5 peers, untrained nurses and midwives, mostly, although the doctor thought of the gulf between him and them as large as that between the captain of an ocean liner and the oarsman of one of the small rowboats that scurry across the Thames.

1. The doctor's attitude towards the "nurses and midwives" in line 5 is best described as
    A) ambivalent
    B) malcontent
    C) placid
    D) vociferous

2. The tour guide was known for both his _____ and his _____: frequently kind, he was also calm and self-assured.
    A) beneficence . . . equanimity
    B) malfeasance . . . placability
    C) complacence . . . equidistance
    D) malignity . . . dexterity

3. Given the gravity of his offenses, the convicted executive displayed astonishing _____ when he addressed the court before sentencing.
    A) invocation
    B) malpractice
    C) volition
    D) placidity

Latin Roots and Feeling Words

Question 4 is based on the passage below.

Pull up to a traffic light in Anytown, U.S.A. and look around. On one side sits an army of national chain stores and "family friendly" restaurants, with names designed to **evoke** memories of small town Americana.

4. In context, "evoke" most nearly means
   A) shout
   B) speak quietly
   C) equal
   D) recall

5. During the Sunday church sermon, the pastor _____ the name of Jesus Christ several times.
   A) provoked
   B) invoked
   C) evoked
   D) advocated

Words in Context

Read each passage and determine the meaning of the words in bold based on the context of the paragraph. Answers can be found on page 37.

The human body is not an ideal model of biological efficiency; it is more like a garbage dump. Buried deep within the genetic code of all humans is the unfortunate record, the genetic "trash," of our less successful evolutionary cousins and ancestors. Consider hemoglobin. Modern human hemoglobin consists of four different protein chains known as globins. Many of the genes that could produce globins are **redundant**, and several others are inactive, damaged in such a way as to make protein production impossible. What is the significance of these **dysfunctional** genes? Quite simply, these damaged genes are the legacy of our less successful ancestors, the biological **remnants** of evolutionary **mutations** that didn't work out well enough.

1. **redundant** _____

_____

2. **dysfunctional** _____

_____

3. **remnant** _____

_____

4. **mutation** _____

_____

While many rivers have long been **utilized** and harnessed by the people who **congregate** near them, the Mekong River, though it snakes through five countries in Southeast Asia, has **eluded** human control until recent times. The low water level in dry seasons **impedes** travel down the river, as does the Mekong's habit of splitting into wide networks of smaller channels. Annual flooding during the monsoon season **thwarts** attempts at long-term agriculture. But in recent years, modern technology and **burgeoning** human populations have begun to **encroach** upon the Mekong's independence. Soon, the Mekong may be as readily **manipulated** as many of its peers around the world.

5. **utilize** _____

_____

6. **congregate** _____

_____

7. **elude** _____

_____

8. **impede** _____

_____

9. **thwart** _____

_____

10. **burgeoning** _____

_____

11. **encroach** _____

_____

12. **manipulate** _____

_____

Crossword Puzzle

Try this crossword as test of your word knowledge. All answers are words found in this chapter. Answers can be found on page 38.

Across

1. a blessing
2. one who performs an act of kindness
5. vague, unclear
6. to deliberately mislead or confuse
10. to call upon a higher power

Down

3. a general sense of unease
4. equally skilled with both hands
7. to speak or act on someone else's behalf
8. to cause
9. unable to be stopped

Chapter 2 Answer Key

Chapter 1 Review

1. A moral person does right; an immoral person does wrong; an **amoral** person _does not care about morality_.
2. Ed's art teacher said that his sculpture was **amorphous**; it was _without shape._
3. John D. Rockefeller was a **magnate**. _Magna-_ means _great_, so a magnate is a _big or important_ person.
4. Every night, Dr. Jekyll underwent a bizarre **metamorphosis**: He _changed_ into Mr. Hyde.
5. When Lucy was a small child, she thought her parents were **omniscient**. Now that she's a teenager, she realizes that they don't know _everything_.
6. Your **peripheral** vision is your ability to see _on the edges (of your vision)._

Fill in the Blank

1. Placid
2. maleficent _or_ malicious _or_ malevolent
3. beneficiary
4. volition
5. implacable
6. advocate
7. equilateral
8. vociferous
9. equitable
10. malpractice

Multiple Choice

1. **B** The best clues here are "shabby" and "untrained." The doctor looks down on his colleagues. Based on what you read in this chapter, (A) means torn between two emotions, (C) means calm, and (D) means loud or talkative. None of these are good matches, so you are left with (B).

2. **A** The clue words for the blanks are "kind" and "calm." *Bene-* means kind or good, while *equ-* implies having an "even" personality. The answer is (A).

3. **D** "Astonishing" is an important word to notice here. The executive's offenses are "grave," so we would expect him to be remorseful. Instead, he must be either unremorseful or calm. Choice (D) means calmness, so it is the correct answer.

4. **D** Hopefully you remembered from the chapter that *–voc* relates to speaking. Eliminate (C). Choices (A) and (B) are good traps, but neither one really describes memories. In context, it would make more sense to "recall," or remember, memories. They are "called forth" in your mind. Choice (D) is correct.

5. **B** This question is tricky, since all of the roots in the answer choices identical. Choice (A) is almost always negative, though, so it wouldn't fit the context. Choice (D) doesn't fit, since you would not *advocate* (speak on someone else's behalf) a name. Choices (B) and (C) are close. Since this is a sermon, (B) is slightly better. *Invoking* implies calling out verbally.

Words in Context

1. **redundant:** unnecessarily repetitive
2. **dysfunctional:** not functioning well
3. **remnant:** leftover
4. **mutation:** change
5. **utilize:** to use
6. **congregate:** to assemble
7. **elude:** to avoid
8. **impede:** to block
9. **thwart:** to stop
10. **burgeoning:** growing rapidly
11. **encroach:** to advance beyond proper limits
12. **manipulate:** to operate in a skillful manner

Crossword Puzzle

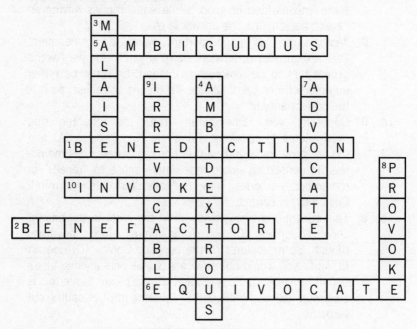

Across

1. a blessing
2. one who performs an act of kindness
5. vague, unclear
6. to deliberately mislead or confuse
10. to call upon a higher power

Down

3. a general sense of unease
4. equally skilled with both hands
7. to speak or act on someone else's behalf
8. to cause
9. unable to be stopped

Chapter 2 Word List

Here is an alphabetical list of the most important words you learned in this chapter.

ADVOCATE (AD vuh kut) *n*   a person who argues in favor of a position
- Lulu believes in eliminating tariffs and import restrictions; she is an *advocate* of free trade.

Advocate (AD vuh kayt) can also be a verb:
- The representative of the paint company *advocated* cleaning the deck before painting it, but we were in a hurry so we painted right over the dirt.

Advocacy (AD vuh kuh see) is support of or agreement with a position.

AMBIGUOUS (am BIG yoo us) *adj*   unclear in meaning; confusing; capable of being interpreted in different ways
- The poem we read in English class was *ambiguous;* no one had any idea what the poet was trying to say.

The noun form is *ambiguity* (am bih GYOO uh tee).

AMBIVALENT (am BIV uh lunt) *adj*   undecided; having opposing feelings simultaneously
- Susan felt *ambivalent* about Alec as a boyfriend. Her frequent desire to break up with him reflected this *ambivalence.*

BENEDICTION (ben uh DIK shun) *n*   a blessing; an utterance of good wishes

In certain church services, a *benediction* is a particular kind of blessing.

In secular usage, the word has a more general meaning:
- Jack and Jill were married without their parents' *benediction;* in fact, their parents had no idea that Jack and Jill had married.

Latin Roots and Feeling Words

The opposite of *benediction* is *malediction* (mal uh DIK shun), which means curse or slander:

- Despite the near-universal *malediction* of critics, the sequel to *Gone with the Wind* became a huge bestseller.

BENEFACTOR (BEN uh fak tur) *n* one who provides help, especially in the form of a gift or donation

A person who gives benefits is a *benefactor*. A person who receives benefits is a *beneficiary*. These two words are often confused.

- If your next-door neighbor rewrites his life insurance policy so that you will receive all his millions when he dies, then you become the *beneficiary* of the policy. He is your *benefactor*.

A *malefactor* (MAL uh fak tur) is a person who does bad things.

BENEVOLENT (beh NEV uh lunt) *adj* generous; kind; doing good deeds

- Giving money to the poor is a *benevolent* act. To be *benevolent* is to bestow benefits. The United Way, like any charity, is a *benevolent* organization.

- *Malevolent* (muh LEV uh lunt) means evil, or wishing to do harm.

BENIGN (bih NYNE) *adj* gentle; not harmful; kind; mild

- The threat of revolution turned out to be *benign;* nothing much came of it.

- Charlie was worried that he had cancer, but the lump on his leg turned out to be *benign*.

BURGEON (BUR jun) *v* to expand; to flourish

- The *burgeoning* weeds in our yard soon overwhelmed the grass.

COMPLACENT (kum PLAY sunt) *adj* self-satisfied; overly pleased with oneself; contented to a fault

- The *complacent* camper paid no attention to the poison ivy around his campsite and ended up in the hospital.

- The football team won so many games that it became *complacent*, leading them to be defeated by the worst team in the league.

- To fall into *complacency* is to become comfortably uncaring about the world around you.

Don't confuse *complacent* with *complaisant* (kum PLAY zunt), which means eager to please.

CONGREGATE (KAHN grih gayt) *v*   to come together
- Protestors were granted permission to *congregate* peacefully on the plaza.

The noun form is *congregation,* which often refers to the membership of a house of worship.
- About half of the *congregation* attended the sunrise service.

DEXTROUS (DEX trus) *adj*   skillful; adroit

Dextrous often, but not always, connotes physical ability. Like *adroit*, it comes from the Latin word for *right* (as in the direction) because right-handed people were once considered physically and mentally superior.
- Ilya was determined not to sell the restaurant; even the most *dextrous* negotiator could not sway him.

You may also see this word spelled *dexterous. Dexterity* is the noun form.

ELUSIVE (ih LOO siv) *adj*   hard to pin down; evasive

To be *elusive* is to *elude,* which means to avoid, evade, or escape.
- The answer to the problem was *elusive;* every time the mathematician thought he was close, he discovered another error. (One could also say that the answer to the problem *eluded* the mathematician.)

ENCROACH (en KROHCH) *v*   to make gradual or stealthy inroads into; to trespass
- As the city grew, it *encroached* on the countryside surrounding it.

- With an *encroaching* sense of dread, I slowly pushed open the blood-spattered door.

- My neighbor *encroached* on my yard by building his new stockade fence a few feet on my side of the property line.

EQUANIMITY (ek wuh NIM uh tee) *n*   composure; calm
- The entire apartment building was crumbling, but Rachel faced the disaster with *equanimity*. She ducked out of the way of a falling beam and continued searching for an exit.

- John's mother looked at the broken glass on the floor with *equanimity*; at least he didn't hurt himself when he knocked over the vase.

EQUITABLE (EK wuh tuh bul) *adj*   fair
- The pirates distributed the loot *equitably* among themselves, so that each pirate received the same share as every other pirate.

- The divorce settlement was quite *equitable*. Sheila got the right half of the house, and Tom got the left half.

Equity is fairness; *inequity* is unfairness. *Iniquity* and *inequity* both mean unfair, but *iniquity* implies wickedness as well. By the way, *equity* is also a finance term used to refer to how much something (usually property or a business) is worth after subtracting what is owed on it, i.e., home equity.

EQUIVOCAL (ih KWIV uh kul) *adj*   ambiguous; intentionally confusing; capable of being interpreted in more than one way

To be *equivocal* is to be intentionally ambiguous or unclear.
- Joe's response was *equivocal;* we couldn't tell whether he meant yes or no, which is precisely what Joe wanted.

- Dr. Festen's *equivocal* diagnosis made us think that he had no idea what Mrs. Johnson had.

To be *equivocal* is to *equivocate*. To *equivocate* is to mislead by saying confusing or ambiguous things:
- When we asked Harold whether that was his car that was parked in the middle of the hardware store, he *equivocated* and asked, "In which aisle?"

EVOKE (i VOHK) *v* to summon forth; to draw forth; to awaken; to produce or suggest

- The car trip with our children *evoked* many memories of similar car trips I had taken with my own parents when I was a child.

- Professor Herman tried repeatedly but was unable to *evoke* any but the most meager response from his students.

- Paula's Christmas photographs *evoked* both the magic and the crassness of the holiday.

The act of *evoking* is called *evocation* (e voh KAY shun).

- A visit to the house in which one grew up often leads to the *evocation* of old memories.

Something that *evokes* something else is said to be *evocative* (i VAHK uh tiv).

- The old novel is highly *evocative* of its era; reading it makes you feel as though you have been transported a hundred years into the past.

IMPEDE (im PEED) *v*   to obstruct or interfere with; to delay

- The faster I try to pick up the house, the more the cat *impedes* me; he sees me scurrying around and, thinking I want to play, he runs up and winds himself around my ankles.

- The fact that the little boy is missing all his front teeth *impedes* his ability to speak clearly.

Something that *impedes* is an *impediment* (im PED uh munt).

- Irene's inability to learn foreign languages was a definite *impediment* to her mastery of French literature.

INVOKE (in VOHK) *v*   to entreat or pray for; to call on as in prayer; to declare to be in effect

- Oops! I just spilled cake mix all over my mother's new kitchen carpet. I'd better go *invoke* her forgiveness.

- This drought has lasted for so long that I'm just about ready to *invoke* the rain gods.

- The legislature passed a law restricting the size of the state's deficit, but it then neglected to *invoke* it when the deficit soared above the limit.

The noun is *invocation* (in vuh KAY shun).

IRREVOCABLE (i REV uh kuh bul) *adj*   irreversible

To *revoke* (ri VOHK) is to take back. Something *irrevocable* cannot be taken back.

- My decision not to wear a Tarzan costume and ride on a float in the Macy's Thanksgiving Day Parade is *irrevocable;* there is absolutely nothing you could do or say to make me change my mind.

- After his friend pointed out that the tattoo was spelled incorrectly, Tom realized that his decision to get a tattoo was *irrevocable.*

MALAISE (ma LAYZ) *n*   a feeling of depression, uneasiness, or queasiness

- *Malaise* descended on the calculus class when the teacher announced a quiz.

MALFEASANCE (mal FEE zuns) *n*   an illegal act, especially by a public official

- President Ford officially pardoned former President Nixon before the latter could be convicted of any *malfeasance.*

PLACATE (PLAY kayt) *v*   to pacify; to appease; to soothe

- The tribe *placated* the angry volcano by tossing a few teenagers into the raging crater.

- The beleaguered general tried to *placate* his fierce attacker by sending him a pleasant flower arrangement. His implacable enemy decided to attack anyway.

PLACEBO (pluh SEE boh) *n*   a fake medication; a fake medication used as a control in tests of the effectiveness of drugs

- Half the subjects in the experiment received the real drug; half were given *placebos.* Of the subjects given *placebos*, 50 percent reported a definite improvement, 30 percent reported a complete cure, and 20 percent said, "Oh, I bet you just gave us a placebo."

- Mrs. Walters is a total hypochondriac; her doctor prescribes several *placebos* a week just to keep her from calling him so often.

REDUNDANT (ri DUN dunt) *adj*   unnecessarily repetitive; excessive; excessively wordy
- Eric had already bought paper plates, so our purchase of paper plates was *redundant*.
- Shawn's article was *redundant*—he kept saying the same thing over and over again.

An act of being *redundant* is a *redundancy*.
- The title "Department of *Redundancy* Department" is *redundant*.

THWART (thwort) *v*   to prevent from being accomplished; to frustrate; to hinder
- I wanted to do some work today, but it seemed as though fate *thwarted* me at every turn; first, someone on the phone tried to sell me a magazine subscription, and then my printer broke down, and then I discovered that my favorite movie was on TV.
- There's no *thwarting* Yogi Bear once he gets it into his mind that he wants a picnic basket; he will sleep until noon, but before it's dark, he'll have every picnic basket that's in Jellystone Park.

VOCIFEROUS (voh SIF ur us)   *adj*   loud; noisy; expressed in a forceful or loud way
- Her opposition to the bill was *vociferous*; she used every opportunity to condemn and protest against it.

VOLITION (voh LISH un) *n*   will; conscious choice
- Insects, lacking *volition,* simply aren't as interesting to the aspiring anthropologist as humans are.
- The jury had to decide whether the killing had been an accident or an act of *volition*.

CHAPTER 3

Greek Roots

Chapter 2 Review

Before beginning Chapter 3, let's see how much you remember from the previous chapter with this fill-in-the-blank exercise. You can check your answers on page 60.

1. The proposed law was a good one, but it didn't pass because it had no **advocate;** no senator stepped forward to _____.

2. We listened to the weather report, but the forecast was **ambiguous**; _____ whether the day was going to be rainy or sunny.

3. A **benediction** is _____; a **malediction** is _____.

4. Batman and Robin _____ the **malefactors** in Gotham City.

5. Karla has a **benign** personality; she is not at all _____.

6. The president of the student council was appalled by the **complacency** of his classmates; not one of the seniors seemed to _____ about the activities of the council.

7. Though not imposing in stature, Rashid was the most **dexterous** basketball player on the court; he often beat taller competitors with his _____ management of the ball.

8. King Solomon's decision was certainly **equitable**; each mother would receive _____ portions of the child.

9. Something that can be _____ is **revocable**.

10. Randy often becomes **vociferous** during arguments. He doesn't know what he believes, but he states it _____ nevertheless.

More Word Roots: It's All Greek to Us

In Chapters 1 and 2, we looked at many examples of Latin's influence on the English language. Now in this chapter we will explore the many ways that the Greek language influenced English. Words with Greek roots show up everywhere in the English language. When you see words containing letter combinations such as *ph-*, *ps-*, or a silent *y*, for example, there is a good chance that word is derived from Greek. Let's look at some examples.

path- emotion

That's **pathetic**! You've probably heard or said that phrase a few times in your life, but what does it *really* mean? *Path-* relates to emotion, so when you tell your little brother that he's *pathetic*, what you're really saying is "I feel for you. I feel bad for you."

The three most important *path-* words you should know are **sympathy**, **empathy**, and **apathy**. *Sym-* and *em-* mean "with," while *a-* means "without." So, you guessed it, *sympathy* and *empathy* mean feeling "with" someone, while *apathy* refers to a lack of emotion. What about **antipathy**? *Anti-* means "against," so *antipathy* is hatred. (English is easy when you know the roots, right?)

> ## The *Path-* to Success
>
> *Path-* shows up in many medical terms. For instance, a **pathology** is a disease. An **osteopath** is a type of medical doctor. We even have **psychopaths** in **psychiatry**. What's the connection? Well, since *path-* relates to emotion, a *path-* in medicine pertains to human suffering (or those who aid in helping it). You are not likely to see many medical *path-* words on the SAT.

anthrop-; andro-; gyn-

> *anthrop-* humans
> *andro-* male
> *gyn-* female

What is **anthropology**? Well, since *–ology* is "the study of," *anthropology* must refer to the study of human civilizations.

You may already know that *mis-* in front of a word indicates a negative meaning. So, a **misanthrope** hates people. **Misogyny** refers specifically to the hatred of women, while **misandry** refers to the hatred of men.

Here are some other important words in this family of roots:

---

androgens (n.)—in biology, male hormones

androgynous (adj.)—relating to something that contains both male and female characteristics, or that has *ambiguous* characteristics

android (n.)—a robot that appears to be human or male

anthropocentric (adj.)—a worldview that tends to put human beings at the center

anthropomorphic (adj.)—a perspective that tends to assign human characteristics to plants or animals

gynecologist (n.)—a medical doctor who specializes in women's health

---

phil- love of

Maybe you learned in geography class that **Philadelphia** is the City of Brotherly Love. That's because *phil-* always indicates love or affection for a person or idea. **Anglophiles** love England. **Francophiles** love France. **Bibliophiles** love books. We could go on. Let's take *phil-* and match it up with some other roots. See if you can guess the meanings. (The answers are found on the next page.)

philanthropy _____

audiophile _____

bibliophile _____

videophile _____

zoophile _____

What kind of "phile" are you? (We're logophiles—look it up!)

philanthropy: generosity; literally, love of humanity

audiophile: one who enjoys recorded music, especially the equipment used to listen to such music

bibliophile: one who loves or collects books

videophile: one who loves television or recorded films

zoophile: one who loves animals or advocates for their protection

---

soph- wisdom

Sophia is a very old Greek word meaning "wisdom." *Soph-* shows up in lots of important words and combines well with some of the roots we've already learned. For instance, **philosophy** is the love (or pursuit) of wisdom. When you say someone is **sophisticated**, you are actually saying that that person has wisdom about the "ways of the world."

But what about **sophomores**? If you are a sophomore in high school, we apologize in advance: It does *not* mean you are wise. It actually means "wise fool." So, someone behaving in a **sophomoric** manner is being immature.

In ancient Greece, the **Sophists** were a group of philosophers who charged money to students to teach them various techniques of argumentation. They developed a reputation as shady characters, so we now think of **sophistry** as a kind of wisdom that seems true but is actually false.

log-; -ology

log-   words
-ology study of

You may already know that *-ology* means "the study of." You see this root constantly in school when talking about disciplines such as **biology**, **psychology**, **anthropology**, and **paleontology**. But no matter the field of study, what are you *really* studying? Words. *Log-* is a Greek root that pertains to words and beliefs. There are so many *log-* words in the English language that we could not possibly cover them all here, but like all roots, you need not memorize hundreds of words. Just get to know the roots and you will be able to guess the meaning (and usually be right).

Logic is the use of words and ideas to persuade or to arrive at truth. *Ana-* means "against," so an **analogy** is an attempt to take two different things and join them together in meaning. Here's an example of an analogy: "*Maple* is to *tree*" as "*sedan* is to *car.*" Trees and cars don't have much to do with each other, but the analogy helps to see their similarity: They are both "types" of something. An **analogous** situation is one that contains some common thread or theme (even though the two things being compared might seem dissimilar). Test writers *love* to test you on this word.

Here are some other *log-* words:

---

catalog (v.)—to place in order or to organize (often by words)

dialogue (n.)—a conversation involving two or more people

eulogy (n.)—a speech of praise, especially given at a funeral

monologue (n.)—a long speech made by one person

neologism (n.)—a new word

prologue (n.)—an introductory chapter or event

---

chron- time

You probably know what it means to put items in **chronological** order: to order words or objects by their place in time. Look at those roots! *Chron-* pertains to time, and we already know what *log-* means. (Turn back to page 53 if you've forgotten already!)

What about an **anachronism**? As we discussed earlier, *ana-* means "against." So, an *anachronism* is something that appears to be out of place in time. If you were watching an old Western movie set in the 1850s, it would be an *anachronism* to see someone driving down the road in a sports car.

Here are some other *chron-* words:

> **chronic** (adj.)—happening over a long period of time
>
> **chronicle** (v.)—to record events, especially in chronological order
>
> **chronometer** (n.)—a timepiece, such as a watch or clock
>
> **synchronized** (adj.), **synchronicity** (n.)—occurring at the same time (*syn-* is "with" or "same")

Chapter 3 Practice Exercises

Roots Review

For each of the following words, circle the root(s) and write down their meanings. Answers can be found on page 61.

1. **amorphous**
   _____

2. **anaerobic**
   _____

3. **antidepressant**
   _____

4. **autobiography**
   _____

5. **coworker**
   _____

6. **contradict**
   _____

7. **decelerate**
   _____

8. **excavate**
   _____

9. **inappropriate**
   _____

10. **magnanimous**
    _____

11. **misbehave**
    _____

12. **nondescript**

_____

13. **omniscience**

_____

14. **peripheral**

_____

15. **postpone**

_____

16. **predict**

_____

17. **rebound**

_____

18. **substandard**

_____

19. **superfluous**

_____

20. **transient**

_____

21. **benevolent**

_____

22. **malice**

_____

23. **ambidextrous**

_____

24. **equivalent**

_____

25. **vocal**

_____

Crossword Puzzle

Try this crossword puzzle as a test of your word knowledge. All answers are words found in this chapter. Answers can be found on page 62.

Across

1. compassion
4. a conversation
5. hatred of women
8. a robot

Down

2. hatred
3. a new word
6. false wisdom
7. similar
9. one who loves music
10. an introductory chapter

Word Search

Find the words from the list below and then write a definition for each word on the lines provided. Answers can be found on page 63.

```
V Q L Q Z R I G H D P E K A I Q H M N O G S J N
E B D K K R U I R F K X X X B W Y S A R V G G V
A N E W R M A L I C I O U S E J O V W U J V F E
A P T B Y C I L P Y W Z U A N E D F M U F S C H
W I P E P V Q D D Y E C H J E W Z S V H C U A D
V K A R E T L M N Z E P Y F F E I X R L E O C C
D Y D U Z E S Y T Y Q C W B A K D B G J M R P L
Y A A T N A T S I D I U Q E C O D N D U J E I Z
J H L L A C O V I U Q E V F T V S O M X Z F P X
Z R A J I M J C O L A W C T O O T R A F A I J V
M U M S F A J P U W V H U M R R L Y U M P C B A
P B V A R M X I S T J C A J N P R P M I B O T N
C L T V Q A X Q X P I M P L A C A B L E Z V S O
D G A N Q L M A L F E A S A N C E Z K V Z Y X I
Y E R C E R W V O I D W T D S Q P H B J T U M T
A A W B A L D T K K V I S G H Y H Y W I Q X J I
Y H R F D T A B E N E F I C I A L O M L Z Q R L
C O S U D E E V E W I X F P T I N I U N U M H O
H T Y R W I L Z I I E N W O C D N P T K L H M V
C V O L Z M W Q V B X W U S S A W K Z D M I M S
H R F K T M G X X B M T O X U Q Q K Q C M G M A
S U O R T X E D I B M A V Q I W B R O U F I W M
T F X N O I T C I D E N E B I L W K G H N Y B S
Z Z S G W J Y E Q L G U B J J H L P Z K Z H B N
```

1. **implacable** _____
2. **vociferous** _____
3. **equivocal** _____
4. **maladapted** _____
5. **benediction** _____
6. **volition** _____
7. **placate** _____
8. **equanimity** _____
9. **ambivalent** _____
10. **malfeasance** _____
11. **benefactor** _____
12. **provoke** _____
13. **equidistant** _____
14. **ambidextrous** _____
15. **malicious** _____
16. **beneficial** _____

Chapter 3 Answer Key

Chapter 2 Review

1. The proposed law was a good one, but it didn't pass because it had no **advocate;** no senator stepped forward to _speak in favor of it._

2. We listened to the weather report, but the forecast was **ambiguous;** _it was unclear_ whether the day was going to be rainy or sunny.

3. A **benediction** is _a blessing;_ a **malediction** is _a curse._

4. Batman and Robin _defeated_ the **malefactors** in Gotham City.

5. Karla has a **benign** personality; she is not at all _cruel; mean._

6. The president of the student council was appalled by the **complacency** of his classmates; not one of the seniors seemed to _care_ about the activities of the council.

7. Though not imposing in stature, Rashid was the most **dexterous** basketball player on the court; he often beat taller competitors with his _skillful_ management of the ball.

8. King Solomon's decision was certainly **equitable;** each mother would receive _equal_ portions of the child.

9. Something that can be _taken back_ is **revocable.**

10. Randy often becomes **vociferous** during arguments. He doesn't know what he believes, but he states it _loudly_ nevertheless.

Roots Review

1. *a-, morph-* : without; change
2. *ana-* : without; against
3. *anti-* : against
4. *auto-* : self
5. *co-* : with
6. *contra-* : against
7. *de-* : remove
8. *ex-* : outside
9. *in-* : not
10. *magna-* : great
11. *mis-* : wrong; bad
12. *non-* : not
13. *omni-* : all
14. *peri-* : around
15. *post-* : after
16. *pre-* : before
17. *re-* : again
18. *sub-* : under
19. *super-* : extra
20. *trans-* : across
21. *bene-, vol-* : good; wishes
22. *mal-* : bad
23. *ambi-* : both
24. *equi-* : equal
25. *voc-* : speak

Crossword Puzzle

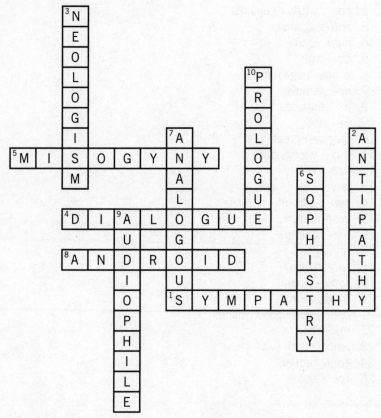

Across

1. compassion
4. a conversation
5. hatred of women
8. a robot

Down

2. hatred
3. a new word
6. false wisdom
7. similar
9. one who loves music
10. an introductory chapter

Word Search

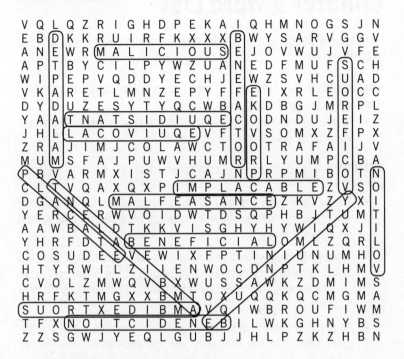

1. **implacable:** unable to be soothed
2. **vociferous:** loud; talkative
3. **equivocal:** deliberately vague; unclear
4. **maladapted:** not well adapted
5. **benediction:** a blessing
6. **volition:** will; desire
7. **placate:** to soothe
8. **equanimity:** a state of calm; composure
9. **ambivalent:** torn between two emotions
10. **malfeasance:** misconduct
11. **benefactor:** a generous person
12. **provoke:** to cause or incite
13. **equidistant:** of equal distance from each other
14. **ambidextrous:** able to use both hands effectively
15. **malicious:** wishing harm on another
16. **beneficial:** of benefit

Chapter 3 Word List

Here is an alphabetical list of the most important words you learned in this chapter.

ANACHRONISM (uh NAK ruh ni zum) *n*   something out of place in time or history; an incongruity
- In this age of impersonal hospitals, a doctor who remembers your name seems like an *anachronism*.

ANALOGY (uh NAL uh jee) *n*   a comparison of one thing to another; similarity
- To say having an allergy feels like being bitten by an alligator would be to make or draw an *analogy* between an allergy and an alligator bite.

- *Analogy* usually refers to similarities between things that are not otherwise very similar. If you don't think an allergy is at all like an alligator bite, you might say, "That *analogy* doesn't hold up."

- To say that there is no *analogy* between an allergy and an alligator bite is to say that they are not *analogous* (uh NAL uh gus).

- Something similar in a particular respect to something else is its *analog* (AN uh lawg), sometimes spelled *analogue*.

ANTHROPOMORPHIC (an thruh puh MOHR fik) *adj*   ascribing human characteristics to nonhuman animals or objects
- This word is derived from the Greek word *anthropos*, which means man or human, and the Greek word *morphos*, which means shape or form.

- To speak of the "hands" of a clock, or to say that a car has a mind of its own, is to be *anthropomorphic*.

- To be *anthropomorphic* is to engage in *anthropomorphism*.

ANTIPATHY (an TIP uh thee) *n*　firm dislike; a dislike
- I feel *antipathy* toward bananas wrapped in ham. I do not want them for dinner. I also feel a certain amount of *antipathy* toward the cook who keeps trying to force me to eat them. My feelings on these matters are quite *antipathetic* (an tip uh THET ik).
- I could also say that ham-wrapped bananas and the cooks who serve them are among my *antipathies*.

APATHY (AP uh thee) *n*　lack of interest; lack of feeling
- The members of the student council accused the senior class of *apathy* because none of the seniors had bothered to sign up for the big fundraiser.
- The word *apathetic* is the adjective form of *apathy*.

CHRONIC (KRAHN ik) *adj*　occurring often and repeatedly over a period of time; lasting a long time
- DJ's *chronic* back pain often kept him from football practice, but the post-game internal bleeding lasted only a day.
- *Chronic* is usually associated with something negative or undesirable: *chronic* illness, *chronic* failure, *chronic* depression. You would be much less likely to encounter a reference to *chronic* success or *chronic* happiness, unless the writer or speaker was being ironic.
- A *chronic* disease is one that lingers for a long time, doesn't go away, or keeps coming back. The opposite of a *chronic* disease is an *acute* disease. An *acute* disease is one that comes and goes very quickly. It may be severe, but it doesn't last very long.

CHRONICLE (KRAHN uh kul) *n*　a record of events in order of time; a history
- Sally's diary provided her mother with a detailed *chronicle* of her daughter 's extracurricular activities.
- *Chronicle* can also be used as a verb: The reporter *chronicled* all the events of the revolution.
- *Chronology* and *chronicle* are nearly synonyms: Both provide a *chronological* list of events. *Chronological* means "in order of time."

EMPATHY (EM puh thee) *n* identification with the feelings or thoughts of another

- Shannon felt a great deal of *empathy* for Bill's suffering; she knew just how he felt.

- To feel *empathy* is to *empathize* (EM puh thyze), or to be *empathic* (em PATH ik): Samuel's tendency to *empathize* with creeps may arise from the fact that Samuel himself is a creep.

- This word is sometimes confused with *sympathy*, which is compassion toward someone or something, and *apathy* (AP uh thee), which means indifference or lack of feeling.

- *Empathy* goes a bit further than sympathy; both words mean that you understand someone's pain or sorrow, but *empathy* indicates that you also feel the pain yourself.

EULOGY (YOO luh jee) *n* a spoken or written tribute to a person, especially a person who has just died

- The *eulogy* Michael delivered at his father's funeral was so moving that it brought tears to the eyes of everyone present.

- To give a *eulogy* about someone is to *eulogize* (YOO luh jyze) that person. Don't confuse this word with *elegy*, which is a mournful song or poem.

MISANTHROPIC (mis un THRAHP ik) *adj* hating mankind

- A *misogynist* (mis AH juh nist) hates women.

- The opposite of a *misanthrope* (MIS un throhp) is a *philanthropist* (fuh LAN thruh pist).

NEOLOGISM (nee OL uh ji zum) *n* a new word or phrase; a new usage of a word

- Some people don't like *neologisms*. They like the words we already have. But at one time every word was a *neologism*. Someone somewhere had to be the first to use it.

PATHOLOGY (puh THAHL uh jee) *n*   the science of diseases
- *Pathology* is the science or study of diseases, but not necessarily in the medical sense.

- *Pathological* means relating to *pathology,* but it also means arising from a disease. So if we say Brad is an inveterate, incorrigible, *pathological* (path uh LAHJ uh kul) liar, we are saying that Brad's lying is a sickness.

PATHOS (PA thos) *n*   that which makes people feel pity or sorrow
- Laura's dog gets such a look of *pathos* whenever he wants to go for a walk that it's hard for Laura to turn him down.

- There was an unwitting *pathos* in the way the elderly shopkeeper had tried to spruce up his window display with crude decorations cut from construction paper.

- Don't confuse *pathos* with *bathos* (BAY thahs). *Bathos* is trite, insincere, sentimental *pathos.*

PHILANTHROPY (fi LAN thruh pee) *n*   love of mankind, especially by doing good deeds
- His gift of one billion dollars to the local orphanage was the finest act of *philanthropy* I've ever seen.

- A charity is a *philanthropic* (fi lun THRAH pik) institution. An *altruist* is someone who cares about other people.

SOPHOMORIC (sahf uh MOHR ik) *adj*   juvenile; childishly goofy
- The dean of students suspended the fraternity's privileges because its members had streaked through the library wearing togas, soaped the windows of the administration building, and engaged in other *sophomoric* antics during Parents' Weekend.

- "I expect the best man to be *sophomoric*—but not the groom. Now, give me that slingshot, and leave your poor fiancée alone!" the minister scolded Andy at his wedding rehearsal.

CHAPTER 4

More Latin
Roots

Chapter 3 Review

Before beginning Chapter 4, let's see how much you remember from the previous chapter with this fill-in-the-blank exercise. You can check your answers on page 86.

1. To be **anthropomorphic** is to see a human _____ (either literally or metaphorically) in things that are not human.

2. My **antipathies** are the things I don't _____.

3. Jill didn't _____ about current events; she was entirely **apathetic**.

4. Someone who _____ comes in last could be called a **chronic** loser.

5. A **misanthropic** person doesn't make distinctions; he or she _____ everyone.

6. Terry said the new novel was _____: filled with **pathos**.

7. A **philanthropist** actively does things to _____ other people.

8. The _____ tenth graders didn't mind being called **sophomoric**; after all, they were sophomores!

Latin Roots, Part 2

The last time we talked about Latin roots was in Chapter 2, in our discussion of feeling words. In this chapter we revisit Latin roots that show up in an abundance of English words you may see on the SAT. As in the previous chapters, each root is accompanied by its meaning, words that contain the root, and example sentences to show you those words in context.

cred-   belief; trust

Chances are your parents have credit cards. Why is it called a **credit** card? Very simply, the bank (**creditor**) that issued your parents that card *believes* or *trusts* that the money borrowed will be paid back eventually.

- In court cases, a **credible** witness is one whom the jury can *believe*.

- If you say, "That's **incredible!**" what you are literally saying is that what you just witnessed was so amazing that you can hardly *believe* that it is true.

Here are some more *cred-* words:

> **credence** (n.)—believability; trustworthiness
>
> **credo** (n.)—a belief or motto
>
> **credulous** (adj.)—eager to believe; gullible
>
> **creed** (n.)—a system of beliefs, especially religious
>
> **incredulous** (adj.)—unwilling to believe

dict- speak; say

Dict- is another Latin root that shows up in so many words we can hardly list them all here. But here we will cover the most important ones—the words you are most likely to see on the SAT. *Dict-* pertains to speaking or saying. So, a **dictionary** is a list of words you would say in a language.

- To **dictate** or make **dictation** is to speak or tell.

- A **dictator** tells others what to do, especially in a forceful way.

- To **contradict** is to say the opposite of what another might say. (*Contra-* means "against.")

- A **prediction** is speaking about events before they actually happen. (*Pre-* means "before.")

> Sometimes the *t* in *dict-* is not present.
> For instance, **indicate** means "to show
> the way," particularly by speaking.

These are words you may already know. Let's take a look at some more challenging uses of *dict-*. Fill in the blanks for the last two words; if you don't know the answers, look back to Chapter 1.

> **diction** (n.)—word choice
>
> **dictum** (n.)—a command
>
> **indict** (v.) (pronounced in DITE)—to formally accuse; to say that someone is guilty
>
> **malediction** (n.) _____
>
> **benediction** (n.) _____

nom- name

If you have ever studied Spanish or French, you may recognize *nom-*. *Nombre* in Spanish means "name," and *nom* has that same meaning in French.

- To **nominate** someone means to "name" or recommend that person for a particular position.

- A **misnomer** is a false name, as in, "This Canadian bacon is made in Nebraska."

Nom- can also masquerade as *nym-*.

- A **pseudonym** is a false name that an author uses, as in, "Samuel Clemen's **pseudonym** was Mark Twain."

Here are some other *nom-* words:

anonymous (adj.)—having an unknown or withheld name (*a-* means "without.")

autonomy (n.)—independence (literally, to "name" the "self" [*auto-*])

denominate (v.)—to give a name to; to designate

eponymous (adj.)—deriving from a similar name (e.g., Adele's first CD was titled *Adele*.)

ignominy (n.)—shame or humiliation (literally, being given a *bad name*)

nomenclature (n.)—a system of assigning names to things

nominal (adj.)—a small or insignificant amount ("in name only")

nov- new

Have you ever played video games? (Some of you have played more than a *nominal* number of them.) What's a **novice**? You might know that a **novice**-level player is just a beginner, someone who is "new" to the game. So, if someone says "That's a **novel** idea!" or "This is an **innovative** product," it does not simply mean that the idea or product is interesting or exciting; it means that the thing is *new*.

Let's look at some more *nov-* words:

> **nouveau riche** (n.; French)—one who has suddenly become rich
>
> **nova** (n.)—a new star
>
> **novelty** (n.)—something new and different
>
> **renovate** (v.)—to make something new again; to repair

dign- worthy; deserving

The most common *dign-* word is **dignity**. To maintain your **dignity** is to uphold a feeling of your own worthiness. A **dignified** person has a strong sense of self, while an **indignity** is an action that is offensive to one's sense of self-worth. What if you are feeling **indignant**? It means something offends you and you are angry; it has offended your dignity. The noun form of this word is **indignation**.

In some words, *dign-* can masquerade as *-dain*.

> **deign** (v.)—to do something that one considers beneath one's dignity
>
> **dignify** (v.)—to raise up the status of; to make worthy
>
> **disdain** (n.)—a feeling of strong dislike or disapproval; (v.)—to scorn or consider something beneath oneself (*dis-* + *-dain*)

ver- **truth**

When a jury in a court case is seeking a **verdict**, it is seeking the "truth" about the guilt or innocence of the accused. As you learned earlier, *-dict* means "words," so a **verdict** is literally "true words." To **verify** is to determine the truth about an issue.

> Occasionally, roots can be quirky. To **prevaricate** is to tell a lie, even though the word looks like it would mean to tell the truth (*ver-*) beforehand (*pre-*).

> **aver** (v.)—to confirm the truth of
>
> **veracity** (n.)—truthfulness
>
> **verisimilitude** (n.)—appearing to be true (literally, "similar to the truth")
>
> **verity** (n.)—truth

loc-, loq- word; speech

You might have noticed that this root looks a lot like *log-*. As you learned in Chapter 3, *log-* pertains to words. You can think of *loc-* and *loq-* as *log-*'s close cousins. They relate to words and speech, too:

- An **eloquent** speaker is well-spoken (sounds like "elegant").

- Actors study **elocution** in order to speak well.

- An **interlocutor** is simply one who takes part in a conversation. (The root *inter-* often pertains to exchanges between people and things.)

culp- blame

Who's the **culprit**? If your teacher asks that question, he is looking for someone to *blame*. Words with the root *culp-* often revolve around guilt or blame.

- If you are **culpable**, you are guilty.

- If you are **exculpated**, you are literally taken "out" of the "blame," or found to be not guilty. "**Mea culpa!**" is a commonly used expression when someone is admitting guilt for a particular action.

ami- love; friendship

If you have studied French or Spanish, you probably remember some *ami-* words such as **amor** (love) or **amiable** (friendly). Here are some English words that look suspiciously similar, and they all mean "loving" or "friendly."

---

amenable (adj.)

amiable (adj.)

amicable (adj.)

amity (n.)

amorous (adj.)

---

luc-, lum-   **light**

At some point in science class, you probably learned that a **translucent** material allows only a certain amount of light to pass through it. Maybe you have heard of people lighting off Chinese **luminaries** (floating lights) on holidays. Did you know that to **illustrate** or **illuminate** an idea or image literally means to shine "light" on it?

Here are some other *luc-* and *lum-* words:

---

elucidate (v.)—to make clear (to shine "light" upon)

lackluster (adj.)—lacking pizazz or inspiration ("lacking light")

lucid (adj.)—clear or sane

luminescent (adj.)—filled with light

luminous (adj.)—radiant, as with light

---

tract- pull

Think about a **tractor**. What does it do? Perhaps a lot of things, but one thing it does well is *pull*. Most *tract-* words do not refer to literally pulling an object, but rather more abstract forms of pulling. Here are some examples:

- A **tractable** person is easily persuaded or mentally "pulled," while an **intractable** person is stubborn.

- To **attract** something is to "pull" it toward you, while something that **detracts** from the situation tends to "pull away" from it.

pug-, pugn- fight, attack

In Chapters 5 and 6, we will have fun with mnemonics and explore how they can be an effective study tool, but for now close your eyes and picture a pug dog in your mind. Not the cute, cuddly kind, but a nasty pug: His teeth are bared, he's straining at the leash, and you are desperately in need of the Dog Whisperer. There. Now you will remember *pug-*, the nastiest of our roots. Here are some common *pug-* words:

impugn (v.)—to attack or accuse

pugilist (n.)—a fighter or boxer

pugnacious (adj.)—eager to fight

repugnant (adj.)—distasteful (literally, the thing is "attacking" you)

temp- time

We all know the word *temporary*. A **temporary** situation is one that lasts for only a short *time.* Many difficult words with *temp-* relate to the concept of time.

---

contemporaneous (adj.)—synonym of *contemporary*

contemporary (adj., n.)—belonging to the same time period (*con + temp* = "with time")

extemporaneous (adj.)—performed with little preparation (*ex + temp* = "outside of time")

tempo (n.)—rate or pace of activity

temporal (adj.)—limited by time; temporary

temporize (v.)—to postpone a decision or waste time

Literary Vocab 101

Some other vocabulary you should know for the SAT are literary terms, which occasionally show up on the Reading section. The most important ones are listed below.

- **analogy:** a comparison between things that have similar features

    - *The programmer drew an analogy between the human brain and the computer.*

- **simile:** a direct comparison of two things using the words *like* or *as*

    - *My love is like a red, red rose.*

- **metaphor:** a literally false statement meant to be taken as a comparison between two things

    - *Juliet is the sun.*

- **personification:** a figure of speech in which human qualities are attributed to an animal, object, or idea

    - *The yellow fog rubs its back on the windowpanes.*

- **hyperbole:** deliberate exaggeration

    - *There are a million questions about literary terms on the SAT.*

- **verbal irony:** the use of words to express the opposite of their literal meaning

    - *So you locked your keys in your car and then set off the alarm pulling on the door handle? Brilliant!*

Continued

Literary Vocab 101—Continued

- **dramatic irony:** when events turn out the opposite of the way those involved expect

    - *A man sells his watch to buy a comb for his wife, only to find that she has sold her hair to a wigmaker in order to buy him a watch chain.*

- **allusion:** casual reference; an incidental mention of something

    - *The president made no allusion to the war in his speech.*

- **rhetoric:** the skilled use of language effectively, persuasively or excessively

    - *The preacher's rhetoric convinced my grandmother to donate all her savings to his church.*

- **characterize:** to describe something by stating its main qualities

    - *In his essay, he characterized the 1960s as a period of radical change.*

- **dramatize:** to express or represent vividly, emotionally, or strikingly, as in a drama

    - *My friend always dramatizes everything that happens to her as if it were the worst thing ever.*

Now try your hand at the practice exercises on the next page.

Chapter 4 Practice Exercises

Fill in the Blank

Choose the word that best completes the meaning of the sentence.
Answers can be found on page 86.

1. Because Stan had been preoccupied during his dynamite juggling
   demonstration, the jury felt that he was not _____ for
   the destruction of the property.
   A) amorphous
   B) nondescript
   C) indiscreet
   D) culpable

2. Sally was full of _____ because Mr. Reeves, our English
   teacher, filled the margins of her term paper with harsh remarks
   about her spelling, grammar, and writing style.
   A) omnipotence
   B) volition
   C) beneficence
   D) malaise

3. Da-Shawn and Harry were fired from the stage crew because their
   constant _____ during the play drowned out the actors
   and ruined the performance.
   A) vociferations
   B) analogies
   C) neologisms
   D) synchronizations

4. The baby kittens were so _____ that the nursery school children were able to pick them up, carry them around by the scruffs of their necks, and dress them up in doll clothes.
A) antipathetic
B) chronic
C) placid
D) misanthropic

5. The applicant's credentials were _____, but I didn't like the color of his necktie so I didn't hire him.
A) credible
B) anachronistic
C) analogous
D) anthropomorphic

6. Walter's skin took on a _____ cast after his exposure to the pool of radioactive wastes.
A) sophomoric
B) pathological
C) luminous
D) philanthropic

7. The police spent seven months working on the crime case but were never able to determine the identity of the _____.
A) nominee
B) pseudonym
C) eponym
D) malefactor

8. The portions at the restaurant were so _____ that immediately after dessert we drove to another restaurant and ordered a second full meal.
A) novel
B) nominal
C) dignified
D) verisimilar

Odd Man Out

Each row below consists of four words, three of which are related in meaning. Circle or underline the word that does not fit. Answers can be found on page 87.

1. benevolent	beneficent	benign	beneficiary
2. maleficent	malicious	malcontent	malevolent
3. ambiguity	clarity	vagueness	equivocality
4. apathy	sympathy	empathy	kindness
5. insubordinate	willful	vociferous	intransigent
6. amoral	apolitical	amorous	atheistic
7. pathology	antipathy	misanthropy	misogyny
8. anthropocentric	analogous	anthropomorphic	anthropological
9. philanthropic	degenerate	magnanimous	generous
10. sophisticated	sophistic	sophomoric	foolish

Word Relationships

Decide whether each pair of words is roughly similar (S) in meaning, roughly opposite (O) in meaning, or unrelated (U) to each other. Answers can be found on page 88.

1. analogous	dissimilar	_____
2. monologue	dialogue	_____
3. malaise	catalog	_____
4. eulogy	praise	_____
5. neologism	logic	_____
6. prologue	conclusion	_____
7. chronological	anachronism	_____
8. chronic	unusual	_____
9. synchronized	chronicled	_____
10. credo	creed	_____

Literary Devices

Each passage below contains an example of a literary device. Read the passage and answer the questions that follow. Answers can be found on page 88.

The following passage is an excerpt from Life on the Mississippi by Mark Twain, published in 1883.

But I had lost something, too. I had lost something which could never be restored to me while I lived. All the grace, the beauty, the poetry had gone out of the majestic river! I still keep in mind a certain wonderful sunset which
5 I witnessed when steamboating was new to me. A broad expanse of the river was turned to blood; in the middle distance the red hue brightened into gold, through which a solitary log came floating, black and conspicuous...

1. The phrase "A broad expanse of the river was turned to blood" (lines 5–6) is an example of
   A) irony
   B) anecdote
   C) metaphor
   D) hyperbole

Extracting the venom from the rattlesnake could be euphemistically described as "hard." If a rattlesnake gave up its venom easily, it could cause problems for the animal itself (leading to the old joke about the snake biting its tongue).
5 The venom collector's job, therefore, is to give the rattle-snake a simulated prey for it to bite and release venom into. This is when "milking a snake," as it is known, is more of an art than a science.

2. The author's use of quotes around "hard" in line 2 suggests that the author believes the word to be
   A) a contradiction
   B) an exaggeration
   C) an allusion
   D) an understatement

Chapter 4 Answer Key

Chapter 3 Review

1. To be **anthropomorphic** is to see a human _quality_ (either literally or metaphorically) in things that are not human.

2. My **antipathies** are the things I don't _like_.

3. Jill didn't _care_ about current events; she was entirely **apathetic**.

4. Someone who _usually_ comes in last could be called a **chronic** loser.

5. A **misanthropic** person doesn't make distinctions; he or she _hates_ everyone.

6. Terry said the new novel was _emotionally touching_: filled with **pathos**.

7. A **philanthropist** actively does things to _help_ other people.

8. The _immature_ tenth graders didn't mind being called **sophomoric**; after all, they were sophomores!

Fill in the Blank

1. **D** The clue is "Because Stan had been preoccupied." Therefore, he would not be held guilty. _Culp-_ means guilt or blame, so (D) is the best choice.

2. **D** The clue is "harsh remarks." The word must be negative in tone. Only (D) fits.

3. **A** What would drown out the actors and "ruin" the performance? Not (B), since analogies are simply comparisons between things. Not (C), a new word. Choice (D) might actually be _good_ for a performance, not ruin it. That leaves you with (A). _Vociferations_ not only pertains to speaking, but also implies that Da-Shawn and Harry are speaking loudly.

4. **C** The "nursery school children were able to pick them up, carry them around by the scruffs of their necks, and dress them up in doll clothes." So, these kittens were very calm. _Plac-_ means "calm."

5. **A** The word *but* indicates a change in direction within the sentence. "I didn't hire him," *but* the applicant must have been good. The only word that is positive in meaning is (A). *Cred-* is related to belief or trust.
6. **B** "Radioactive wastes" do not sound beneficial, so you are looking for the most negative word available. *Lum-* and *phil-* mean "light" and "love," so eliminate (C) and (D). You might remember that *path-* can be a medical term as well as a root indicating feeling. A *pathology* is a disease. This is better than (A). Walter is not *sophomoric*, which means immature.
7. **D** Since a "crime" was committed, you want a negative word. Only (D) fits. *Mal-* is always negative.
8. **B** Since they were still hungry after the first meal, the portions must have been small. They were not new, (A); pertaining to truth, (D); or related to dignity, (C). That leaves (B). *Nominal* literally means "in name only" (*nom-*), meaning small or insignificant.

Odd Man Out

1. beneficiary
2. malcontent
3. clarity
4. apathy
5. vociferous
6. amorous
7. pathology
8. analogous
9. degenerate
10. sophisticated

Word Relationships

1. O
2. O
3. U
4. S
5. U
6. O
7. O
8. O
9. U
10. S

Literary Devices

1. **C** A metaphor is a comparison that does not employ the words *like* or *as*. It is unlikely that a river would *actually* turn to blood, so this must be a metaphor.

2. **D** Generally, when an author puts quotes around a single word, it is either to indicate a direct quote or, as in this case, to show sarcasm. So, "hard" is either an exaggeration, (B), or an understatement, (D). Notice the beginning of the next sentence: "*If* a rattlesnake gave up its venom easily...," which means that it *does not.* This must be an understatement, (D).

Chapter 4 Word List

Here is an alphabetical list of the most important words you learned in this chapter.

AMENABLE (uh MEE nuh bul *or* uh MEH nuh bul) *adj* obedient; willing to give in to the wishes of another; agreeable
- I suggested that Brad pay for my lunch as well as for his own; to my surprise, he was *amenable.*

- The plumber was *amenable* to my paying my bill with jelly-beans, which was lucky, because I had more jellybeans than money.

AMIABLE (AY mee uh bul) *adj* friendly; agreeable
- The drama critic was so *amiable* in person that even the subjects of negative reviews found it impossible not to like her.

Amicable is a similar and related word. Two not very *amiable* people might nonetheless make an *amicable* agreement. *Amicable* means politely friendly, or not hostile. Two countries might trade *amicably* with each other even while technically remaining enemies.
- Julio and Clarissa had a surprisingly *amicable* divorce and remained good friends even after paying their lawyers' fees.

AMOROUS (AM ur us) *adj* feeling loving, especially in a romantic sense; in love; relating to love
- The *amorous* couple made quite a scene in the movie theater, kissing for the duration of the movie.

CREDULOUS (KREJ uh lus) *adj* eager to believe; gullible
- Judy was so *credulous* that she simply nodded happily when Kirven told her he could teach her how to fly. Judy's *credulity* (kri DYOOL uh tee) was limitless.

Credulous should not be confused with *credible*. To be *credible* is to be believable. Almost anything, however incredible, is *credible* to a *credulous* person.
- Larry's implausible story of heroism was not *credible*. Still, *credulous* old Louis believed it.

A story that cannot be believed is *incredible*. If you don't believe that story someone just told you, you are *incredulous*.

If something is *credible*, it may gain *credence* (KREED uns), which means belief or intellectual acceptance:
- No one could prove Frank's theory, but his standing at the university helped it gain *credence*.

A similar word is *creditable*, which means worthy of credit or praise:
- Our record in raising money was very *creditable*; we raised several thousand dollars every year.

CULPABLE (KUL puh bul) *adj* deserving blame; guilty
- We all felt *culpable* when the homeless old man died in the doorway of our apartment building.

A person who is *culpable* (a *culprit*) is one who can be blamed for doing something.

To decide that a person is not *culpable* after all is to *exculpate* (EK skul payt) that person.
- Lou's confession didn't *exculpate* Bob because one of the things that Lou confessed was that Bob had helped him commit the crime.

The opposite of *exculpate* is *inculpate*. To *inculpate* is to accuse someone of something.

DEIGN (dayn) *v* to condescend; to think it in accordance with one's dignity (to do something)
- When I asked the prince whether he would be willing to lend me five bucks for the rest of the day, he did not *deign* to make a reply.

DENOMINATION (di nahm uh NAY shun) *n* a classification; a category name
- Religious *denominations* are religious groups consisting of a number of related congregations. Episcopalians and Methodists represent two distinct Christian *denominations*.

Denomination is often used in connection with currency.
- When a bank robber demands bills in small *denominations*, he or she is demanding bills with low face values: ones, fives, and tens.

DICTUM (DIK tum) *n*   an authoritative saying; an adage; a maxim; a proverb
- "No pain, no gain" is a hackneyed *dictum* of sadistic coaches everywhere.

ELOCUTION (el uh KYOO shun) *n*   the art of public speaking
- The mayor was long on *elocution* but short on execution; he was better at making promises than at carrying them out.

- Professor Jefferson might have become president of the university if he had had even rudimentary skills of *elocution*.

A *locution* (loh KYOO shun) is a particular word or phrase. Someone who speaks well is *eloquent* (EL uh kwent).

IGNOMINY (IG nuh min ee) *n*   deep disgrace
- After the big scandal, the formerly high-flying investment banker fell into a life of shame and *ignominy*.

- The *ignominy* of losing the spelling bee was too much for Arnold, who decided to give up spelling altogether.

Something that is deeply disgraceful is *ignominious* (ig nuh MIN ee us):
- Lola's plagiarizing of Nabokov's work was an *ignominious* act that got her suspended from school for two days.

IMPUGN (im PYOON) *v*   to attack, especially to attack the truth or integrity of something
- The critic *impugned* the originality of Jacob's novel, claiming that long stretches of it had been lifted from the work of someone else.

- Fred said I was *impugning* his honesty when I called him a dirty liar, but I told him he had no honesty to *impugn*. This just seemed to make him angrier.

More Latin Roots   **91**

IMPUNITY (im PYOO nuh tee) *n* freedom from punishment or harm
- All students were expected to follow the rules with the exception of the headmaster's son, who was treated with *impunity*; no matter how many rules he broke, he never got detention.

INDICT (in DYTE) *v* to charge with a crime; to accuse of wrongdoing
- After a five-day water fight, the entire freshman dorm was *indicted* on a charge of damaging property.

- The mob boss had been *indicted* many times, but he had never been convicted because his high-priced lawyers had always been able to talk circles around the district attorney.

An act of *indicting* is an *indictment*.
- The broken fishbowl and missing fish were a clear *indictment* of the cat.

INDIGNANT (in DIG nunt) *adj* angry, especially as a result of something unjust or unworthy; insulted
- Ted became *indignant* when the policewoman accused him of stealing the nuclear weapon.

- Isabel was *indignant* when we told her all the nasty things that Blake had said about her over the public address system.

INTRACTABLE (in TRAK tuh bul) *adj* uncontrollable; stubborn; disobedient
- Lavanya was *intractable* in her opposition to pay increases for the library employees; she swore she would never vote to give them a raise.

- The disease was *intractable.* None of the dozens of medicines the doctor tried had the slightest effect on it.

The opposite of *intractable* is *tractable.*

LUCID (LOO sid) *adj* clear; easy to understand
- The professor's explanation of the theory of relativity was so astonishingly *lucid* that even I could understand it.

- The extremely old man was *lucid* right up until the moment he died; his body had given out but his mind was still going strong.

To *elucidate* something is to make it clear, to explain it.

LUMINOUS (LOO muh nus) *adj*   giving off light; glowing; bright
- The moon was a *luminous* disk in the cloudy nighttime sky.
- The dial on my watch is *luminous;* it casts a green glow in the dark.

NOMENCLATURE (NOH mun klay chur) *n*   a set or system of names; a designation; a terminology
- I'd become a botanist in a minute, except that I'd never be able to memorize all of that botanic *nomenclature*.
- In the Bible, Adam created a *nomenclature* when he gave all of the animals names. You could call him the world's first *nomenclator* (NOH mun klay tur). A *nomenclator* is a giver of names.

NOMINAL (NOM uh nul) *adj*   in name only; insignificant
- Bert was the *nominal* chair of the committee, but Sue was the one who ran things.
- The cost was *nominal* in comparison with the enormous value of what you received.

Nominal is also used to mean "A-OK" during rocket launches:
- "All systems are *nominal*," said the NASA engineer as the space shuttle successfully headed into orbit.

NOVEL (NAHV ul) *adj*   fresh; original; new
- Ray had a *novel* approach to homework: He did the work before the teacher assigned it.

PSEUDONYM (SOO duh nim) *n*   a false name; an alias
- Dr. Seuss was the *pseudonym* of Theodor Seuss Geisel.
- The philandering couple used *pseudonyms* when they checked into the hotel for the afternoon because they didn't want anyone to know what they were up to.
- "I'm going to use a *pseudonym* so as not to attract people's attention when I go out in public," announced the famous actor. "I'll call myself Rumblebumble Wart."

The prefix *pseudo-* (SOO doh) means "false." A *pseudointellectual* is someone who pretends to be interested in intellectual things.

REPUGNANT (ri PUG nunt) *adj*   repulsive; offensive; disgusting
- The thought of striking out on his own is absolutely *repugnant* to Allan; he would much prefer to continue living in his old room, driving his parents' car, and eating meals prepared by his mother.

TEMPORAL (TEM pur ul) *adj*   pertaining to time; pertaining to life or earthly existence; non-eternal; short-lived
- Jet lag is a kind of *temporal* disorientation; rapid travel across several time zones can throw off a traveler's sense of time.
- Why is it that *temporal* pleasures seem so much more fun than eternal ones? I'd rather eat a hot-fudge sundae than sit on a cloud playing a harp.
- As the rich old man approached ninety, he grew less concerned with *temporal* matters and devoted more and more energy to deciding which of his children should be left out of his will.

TEMPORIZE (TEM puh ryze) *v*   to stall; to cause delay through indecision
- An important skill required of television newscasters is an ability to *temporize* during technical difficulties so that viewers don't become bored and switch channels.
- The co-op board was afraid to tell the actress flat out that they didn't want her to buy an apartment in their building, so they *temporized* by saying they had to look into some building restrictions first.
- "All right, all right, I'll open the safe for you," Clarence *temporized*, hoping that the police would arrive soon. "But in order to do it, I'll need lots of hot water and some birthday candles."

VERACITY (vuh RAS uh tee) *n*   truthfulness
- The *veracity* of the story of young George Washington chopping down the cherry tree is questioned by serious historians.

Veracious (vuh RAY shus) means truthful.

SAT Power Vocab

VERISIMILITUDE (ver uh si MIL uh tood) *n* similarity to reality; the appearance of truth; looking like the real thing
- They used pinecones and old truck tires to make statues of Hollywood celebrities that were remarkable for their *verisimilitude.*
- The *verisimilitude* of counterfeit eleven-dollar bills did not fool the eagle-eyed treasury officer, who recognized them immediately for what they were.

VERITY (VER uh tee) *n* the quality of being true; something true
- You could hardly doubt the *verity* of her story, especially when she had documents to prove her point.

Many truth-related words derive from the Latin root *verus,* which means "true." *Verisimilar* (ver i SIM uh lur) means having the appearance of truth, and *verisimilitude* (ver i si MIL uh tood) is the quality of being *verisimilar.*
- The plastics company had found a way to make fake leather of shocking *verisimilitude.*

Veracious (vur AY shus) means habitually truthful.

To *aver* (uh VUR) is to state with confidence, as though you know it to be the truth.
- "Yes, that's the man," Charlotte *averred.* "I recognize him for sure."

To *verify* (VER i fye) is to prove that something is true, to confirm it.
- The police were able to *verify* Olin's claim that he had been out of the country at the time of the crime, so they let him go.

PART II

Mnemonic Devices

CHAPTER 5

Mnemonics

Chapter 4 Review

Before beginning Chapter 5, let's see how much you remember from the previous chapter with this fill-in-the-blank exercise. You can check your answers on page 136.

1. Our **amiable** guide made us feel _____ in what would otherwise have been a cold and forbidding museum.

2. The **credulous** housewife _____ that she had won a million dollars through an e-mail scam.

3. The accountant's _____ made him **culpable** in the tax-fraud case.

4. In **elocution** class, Brad learned _____.

5. Babies can mash food into their hair with **impunity**; no one _____ them.

6. The **intractable** child was _____ to his nursery school teacher.

7. Hubert's remarks were few but **lucid**: He _____ the complicated issue with just a handful of well-chosen words.

8. The snow on the ground appeared eerily **luminous** at night; it seemed to _____.

9. It would be easier to trust Charlotte if she had a reputation for being **veracious**—but she doesn't. In fact, she's been called a _____ many times before.

What Are Mnemonics?

A **mnemonic**, or a **mnemonic device**, is a pattern in letters, sounds, or ideas that helps you remember something—in this case, vocabulary. Mnemonics can be a powerful tool when it comes to remembering the meanings of words and incorporating those words into your vocabulary. Whether you realize it or not, you use mnemonics all the time. When you make up a little game to remember your locker combination or a friend's birthday, for example, you're using a mnemonic.

How Do Mnemonics Work?

All mnemonics work in the same way—by helping you to associate what you're trying to remember with something that you already know, or with something that is easier to memorize. Patterns and rhymes are easy to memorize, which explains why so many mnemonics use them. Incidentally, this may also explain why rhyming became a part of poetry. The earliest poets and balladeers didn't write down their compositions because many didn't know how to write. Instead, they memorized them, a task made easier by (among other things) the rhymes at the end of lines.

Don't worry; we're not suggesting that you mentally compose a poem about every new word you learn. Our strategy involves associating a word with a mental image that will, in turn, help you remember the definition of the word. Let's take the word *abridge*, for example, which means to shorten or condense. What image pops into your mind when you think of the word *abridge*? That's easy: a bridge. Now you need to picture something happening on or to that bridge that will help you remember the meaning of the word *abridge*. Your goal is to create a vivid and memorable image in your mind so that the next time you encounter *abridge* in your reading, you'll instantly remember what it means.

To be useful, your image should have something to do with the meaning of the word rather than merely with the way it sounds or looks. If you merely think of a bridge when you see *abridge,* you won't help yourself remember the meaning of the word. What you need is an image that suggests shortening or condensing: a dinosaur taking a big bite out of the middle of a bridge? Carpenters sawing it? The image you choose is up to you.

Let's take another word: *gregarious,* which means sociable, enjoying the company of others. What image springs to mind? Really think now.

Can't think of an image? Be creative. A party animal is *gregarious.* How about imagining a party animal named Greg Arious? Don't stop with his name. You need a picture. So give Greg a funny hat, a noisemaker, and some polka-dot dancing shoes. Or put a lampshade on his head. Think of something that will make you think of sociability the next time you see Greg's name in a book or a magazine. The more real you make Greg Arious seem in your imagination, the less trouble you'll have remembering the meaning of *gregarious.*

Mnemonic devices work best when you have to struggle a little to come up with them. When you create a mnemonic that really means something to you, it will likely become a permanent part of your memory.

SAT Power Vocab's
Suggested Mnemonics

Now let's dive into some fun mnemonics. Remember, if these mnemonic devices don't work for you, you can always make your own.

acute (uh KYOOT) *adj*   sharp; shrewd; discerning

Mnemonic:

In geometry, **ACUTE** angles (less than 90 degrees) are SHARP and pointy.

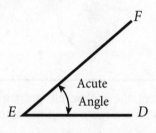

- If your eyesight is *acute,* you can see things that other people can't (e.g., *sharp* eyesight). You have visual *acuity* (uh KYOO uh tee).

- An *acute* mind is a quick, intelligent one (e.g., *sharp* intellect). You have mental *acuity.*

- An *acute* pain is a *sharp* pain.

- *Acute* is a word doctors throw around quite a bit. An *acute* disease is one that reaches its greatest intensity very quickly and then goes away. What could a disease be if it isn't *acute*? See ***chronic***.

> *Acute* means sharp only in a figurative sense. A knife, which is sharp enough to cut, is never said to be *acute*.

anecdote (AN ik doht) *n* a short account of a humorous or revealing incident; a story

Mnemonic:

If you end up with DOTS on your NECK, there must be a STORY to tell.

- The old lady kept the motorcycle gang thoroughly amused with *anecdote* after *anecdote* about her cute little dog.

- Alvare told an *anecdote* about the time Jessica got her big toe stuck in a bowling ball.

- The vice president set the crowd at ease with a touching *anecdote* about his childhood desire to become a public servant.

- To say that the evidence of life on other planets is merely *anecdotal* is to say that we haven't captured any aliens, but simply have heard a lot of stories from people claiming to have been kidnapped by flying saucers.

anomaly (uh NAHM uh lee) *n* an unusual occurrence; an irregularity; a deviation

---

Mnemonics:

- Making an OMELETTE for breakfast on a school day would be an **ANOMALY**. (No time!)
- **ANOMALY** sounds like ABNORMALITY.

- A snowy winter day is not an *anomaly*, but a snowy July day is.

- A house without a roof is an *anomaly*—a cold, wet *anomaly*.

- A roofless house could be said to be *anomalous*. Something that is *anomalous* is something that is not normal or regular.

> Major bonus points to you if you recognized that *anomaly* is really the product of two roots: *ana-* and *nom-*.

apprehensive (ap ruh HEN siv) *adj*   worried; anxious

Mnemonic:

Whenever the farmer came to the barn with a butchering knife, the HEN became FEARFUL.

- The *apprehensive* child clung to his father's leg as the two of them walked into the main circus tent to watch the lion tamer.

- Rhea was *apprehensive* about the exam because she had forgotten to go to class for several months. As it turned out, her *apprehensions* were justified. She couldn't answer a single question on the test.

A *misapprehension* is a misunderstanding:
- Rhea had no *misapprehensions* about her lack of preparation; she knew perfectly well she would fail horribly.

brevity (BREV i tee) *n* the quality or state of being brief in duration

---

Mnemonic:

BREVITY sounds like BRIEF-ITY.

- The audience was deeply grateful for the *brevity* of the after-dinner speaker's remarks.

- The reader of this book may be grateful for the *brevity* of this example.

Brevity is related to the word *abbreviate*.

candor (KAN dur) *n* truthfulness; sincere honesty

Mnemonic:

The child screamed to his mother with much CANDOR that he WANTED the CANDY.

- My best friend exhibited *candor* when he told me that for many years now he has believed me to be a jerk.

- Teddy appreciated Ross's *candor;* Teddy was glad to know that Ross thought Teddy's sideburns looked stupid.

To show *candor* is to be *candid.* To be *candid* is to speak frankly.

- What is *candid* about *candid* photos? The photos are *candid* because they are truthful in showing what people do.

- *Candid* does *not* mean concealed or hidden, even though the camera on the old television show *Candid Camera* was concealed.

conspicuous (kun SPIK yoo us) *adj* easily seen; impossible to miss

---

Mnemonic:

You CAN SPEAK about something CONSPICUOUS because it is OBVIOUS.

- There was a *conspicuous* absence of good food at the terrible party, and many of the guests went out to a restaurant afterward.

- The former president made a *conspicuous* display of his gleaming wristwatch; he had just signed a promotional contract with the watch's manufacturer.

- *Conspicuous* consumption is a variety of showing off that consists of making a public display of buying and using a lot of expensive stuff.

The opposite of *conspicuous* is *inconspicuous.*

deference (DEF ur uns) *n* submission to another's will; respect; courtesy

Mnemonic:

When there is a DIFFERENCE between your rank and that of the person above you (boss/employee, parent/child, teacher/student), you will show DEFERENCE.

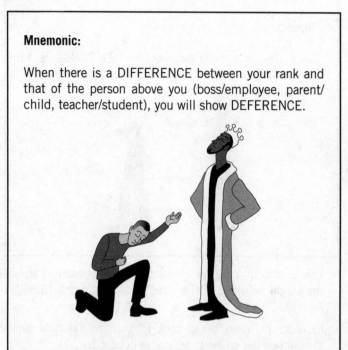

To show *deference* to another is to place that person's wishes ahead of your own.

- Dean showed *deference* to his grandfather: He let the old man have first dibs on the birthday cake.

- Danny stopped texting at the dinner table in *deference* to the wishes of his mother.

To show *deference* to another is to *defer* to that person.

- Joe was supposed to go first, but he *deferred* to Steve, who had been waiting longer.

To show *deference* is also to be *deferential* (def uh REN shul).

- Joe was being *deferential* when he allowed Steve to go first.

denounce (di NOWNS) *v* to condemn openly

Mnemonic:

Since *DE-* is a negative root, to DENOUNCE is to ANNOUNCE something negative about another person.

- The president publicly *denounced* but privately celebrated the illegal activities of the director of the Central Intelligence Agency.

- In order to avoid being sent to jail, the political prisoner *denounced* the cause in which he believed.

An act of *denouncing* is a *denunciation* (di nun see AY shun).

despondent (dih SPAHN dunt) *adj* extremely depressed; full of despair

---

Mnemonic:

A happy person RESPONDS with joy; a DESPONDENT person is not RESPONDING well (to life).

- The cook became *despondent* when the wedding cake fell on the floor fifteen minutes before the reception.

- After the death of his wife, the man was *despondent* for many months.

- The team fell into *despondency* after losing the state championship game by a single point.

disparage (dih SPAR ij) *v* to belittle; to say uncomplimentary things about, often in a somewhat indirect way

Mnemonic:

If you DISplay RAGE at someone you DISlike, you DISPARAGE them.

- The mayor *disparaged* our efforts to beautify the town square when he said that the flowerbed we had planted looked somewhat worse than the bed of weeds it had replaced.

- My guidance counselor *disparaged* my high school record by telling me that not everybody belongs in college.

dubious (DOO bee us) *adj*   full of doubt; uncertain

Mnemonic:

The word DOUBT has a silent *B* in it, so DUBIOUS means DOUBTFUL.

- I was fairly certain that I would be able to fly if I could merely flap my arms hard enough, but Mary was *dubious;* she said I'd better flap my legs as well.

- We were *dubious* about the team's chance of success and, as it turned out, our *dubiety* (doo BYE uh tee) was justified: The team lost.

Dubious and *doubtful* don't mean exactly the same thing. A *dubious* person is a person who has doubts. A *doubtful* outcome is an outcome that isn't certain to occur.

- Sam's chances of getting the job were *doubtful* because the employer was *dubious* of his claim that he had been president of the United States while in high school.

Something beyond doubt is *indubitable.* A dogmatic person believes his opinions are *indubitable.*

empirical (em PIR uh kul) *adj* relying on experience or observation; not merely theoretical

---

Mnemonics:

- Marco Polo KNEW about the Chinese EMPIRE because he EXPERIENCED it and OBSERVED it himself.

- Good UMPIRES must make EMPIRICAL decisions.

- The apple-dropping experiment gave the scientists *empirical* evidence that gravity exists.

- Nicky's idea about the moon being made of pizza dough was not *empirical*.

- We proved the pie's deliciousness *empirically:* by eating it.

explicit (ik SPLIS it) *adj*   clearly and directly expressed

Mnemonic:

"PLEASE SIT and let me EXPLAIN things CLEARLY."

- The graphic and *explicit* movie received an R-rating.
- The machine's instructions were *explicit*: They told us exactly what to do.
- No one *explicitly* asked us to set the barn on fire, but we got the impression that that was what we were supposed to do.

Implicit means indirectly expressed or implied.
- Gerry's dissatisfaction with our work was *implicit* in his expression, although he never criticized us directly.

_Ex_plicit vs. _Im_plicit

We already know from Chapter 1 that *ex-* means "outside" and *im-* or *in-* can mean "inside." *Explicit* information is obvious ("on the outside"), while *implicit* information is hidden or implied ("on the inside").

indifferent (in DIF ur unt) *adj*   not caring one way or the other; apathetic; mediocre

---

Mnemonic:

If you DON'T CARE about something, there will be NO DIFFERENCE in your opinion.

- Pedro was *indifferent* about politics; he didn't care who was elected to office so long as no one passed a law against Monday Night Football.
- We planted a big garden, but the results were *indifferent;* only about half of the flowers came up.
- The painter did an *indifferent* job, but it was good enough for Susan, who was *indifferent* about painting.

The noun is *indifference*:
- Henry's *indifference* was extremely annoying to Melissa, who loved to argue but found it difficult to do so with people who had no opinions.

inept (in EPT) *adj*   clumsy; incompetent

Mnemonic:

Since an APTitude is a skill, to be INEPT is to lack skill.

IN (not) + *APT* (skill) = INEPT

- Joshua is an *inept* dancer; he is as likely to stomp on his partner's foot as he is to step on it.
- Julia's *inept* attempt at humor drew only groans from the audience.

To be *inept* is to be characterized by *ineptitude*, which is the opposite of *aptitude*.

- The woodworking class's *ineptitude* was broad and deep; there was little that they were able to do and nothing that they were able to do well.

The opposite of *inept* is *adept* (uh DEPT).

lament (luh MENT) *v*   to mourn

- From the balcony of the bullet-pocked hotel, the foreign correspondents could hear hundreds of women and children *lamenting* the fallen soldiers.
- As the snowstorm gained in intensity, Stan *lamented* his decision that morning to dress in shorts and a T-shirt.

Lamentable (LAM en tuh bul) or (luh MEN tuh bul) means "regrettable."

malleable (MAL ee uh bul) *adj*   easy to shape or bend

Mnemonic:

Something MELTABLE is MALLEABLE; it can be RE-SHAPED.

- Modeling clay is very *malleable.* So is Stuart. We can make him do whatever we want him to do

mediate (MEE dee ayt) *v*   to help settle differences

Mnemonic:

In math, the MEDIAN is the MIDDLE number in a set, so to MEDIATE is to help two parties meet in the MIDDLE and settle a dispute.

- The United Nations representative tried to *mediate* between the warring countries, but the soldiers just kept shooting at one another.

- Joe carried messages back and forth between the divorcing husband and wife in the hope of *mediating* their differences.

To *mediate* is to engage in *mediation*. When two opposing groups, such as a trade union and the management of a company, try to settle their differences through *mediation,* they call in a *mediator* to listen to their cases and to make an equitable decision.

mercurial (mur KYOOR ee ul) *adj* emotionally unpredictable; rapidly changing in mood

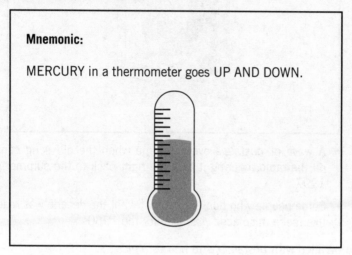

Mnemonic:

MERCURY in a thermometer goes UP AND DOWN.

- A person with a *mercurial* personality is one who changes rapidly and unpredictably between moods.

- *Mercurial* Helen was crying one minute, laughing the next.

nostalgia (nahs TAL juh) *n* sentimental longing for the past; homesickness

Mnemonic:

A NOSTALGIC view of the past means that you have NO TRAGIC memories, only good ones.

- A wave of *nostalgia* overcame me when the old song came on the radio; hearing it took me right back to the summer of 1997.
- Some people who don't remember what the decade was really like feel a misplaced *nostalgia* for the 1950s.

To be filled with *nostalgia* is to be *nostalgic*:
- As we talked about the fun we'd had together in junior high school, we all began to feel a little *nostalgic*.

objective (ahb JEK tiv) *adj*   unbiased; unprejudiced

Mnemonic:

When you look at things as though they are merely OBJECTS, you are able to stay OBJECTIVE.

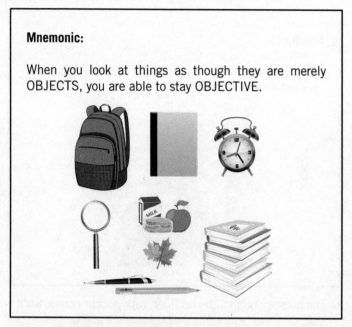

- It's hard for me to be *objective* about her musical talent because she's my daughter.

- Although the judges at the automobile show were supposed to make *objective* decisions, they displayed a definite bias against cars with tacky hood ornaments.

The opposite of *objective* is *subjective*.

Someone who is *objective* is said to have *objectivity* (ahb jek TIV uh tee).

Objective can also be a noun, in which case it refers to a goal, destination, or aim.
- My life's one *objective* is to see that my father never embarrasses me in public again.

obscure (ub SKYOOR) *adj*   unknown; hard to understand; dark

---

Mnemonic:

"OH, is there a CURE for this terrible disease?"
"It's unknown."

- The comedy nightclub was filled with *obscure* comedians who stole one another's jokes and seldom got any laughs.

- The artist was so *obscure* that even his parents had trouble remembering his name.

- The noted scholar's dissertation was terribly *obscure;* it had to be translated into layman's terms before anyone could make heads or tails of it.

- Some contemporary poets apparently believe that the only way to be great is to be *obscure.*

- The details of the forest grew *obscure* as night fell.

The state of being *obscure* in any of its senses is called *obscurity.*

ominous (AHM uh nus) *adj* threatening; menacing; portending doom

---

Mnemonics:

- "OH, MINUS! Something OMINOUS is about to happen."
- OMINOUS sounds like MENACE.

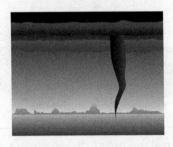

- The sky looks *ominous* this afternoon; there are black clouds in the west, and I think it is going to rain.
- Mrs. Lewis's voice sounded *ominous* when she told the class that it was time for a "little test."

Ominous is related to *omen*.

pervade (pur VAYD) *v*   to spread throughout

Mnemonic:

PERVADE sounds like INVADE.

- A terrible smell *pervaded* the apartment building after the sewer main exploded.
- On examination day, the classroom was *pervaded* by a sense of imminent doom.

Something that *pervades* is *pervasive*:
- There was a *pervasive* feeling of despair on Wall Street on the day the Dow-Jones industrial average fell more than 500 points.
- There was a *pervasive* odor of mold in the house, and we soon discovered why: The basement was filled with the stuff.

prudent (PROOD unt) *adj*   careful; having foresight

> **Mnemonic:**
>
> A PROUD STUDENT is PRUDENT and careful about her schoolwork.
>
>

- Joe is a *prudent* money manager. He doesn't invest heavily in racehorses, and he puts only a small part of his savings in the office football pool. Joe is the epitome of *prudence*.

The opposite of *prudent* is *imprudent:*

- It was *imprudent* of us to pour gasoline all over the floor of our living room and then light a fire in the fireplace.

reciprocal (ri SIP ruh kul) *adj*   mutual; shared; interchangeable

---

Mnemonic:

In math, the RECIPROCAL of a number is its MIRROR image; the numbers SHARE similarities.

$$\frac{6}{8} \text{ reciprocal is } \frac{8}{6}$$

- The Rochester Club had a *reciprocal* arrangement with the Duluth Club. Members of either club had full privileges of membership at the other.
- Their hatred was *reciprocal;* they hated each other.

To *reciprocate* is to return in kind, to interchange, or to repay.
- Our new neighbors had had us over for dinner several times, but we were unable to *reciprocate* immediately because our dining room was being remodeled.

Reciprocity (res uh PRAHS uh tee) is a *reciprocal* relation between two parties, often whereby both parties gain.

resignation (rez ig NAY shun) *n*   passive submission; acquiescence

---

Mnemonic:

After the employee was asked to RESIGN, she left her job in depressed RESIGNATION.

- No one had expected that Warren would take being kicked off the team with so much *resignation*; he simply hung up his uniform and walked sadly out of the locker room.

- There was *resignation* in Alex's voice when he announced at long last that there was nothing more that he could do.

To exhibit *resignation* is to be *resigned* (ri ZYNDE). Note carefully this particular meaning of the word.
- After collecting several hundred rejection slips, Darla finally *resigned* herself to the fact that her novel would never be published.

substantiate (sub STAN shee ayt) *v*   to prove; to verify; to confirm

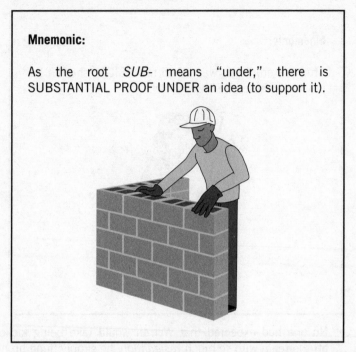

Mnemonic:

As the root *SUB-* means "under," there is SUBSTANTIAL PROOF UNDER an idea (to support it).

- Experts from the transit department were unable to *substantiate* the woman's assertion that little men from the center of the Earth had invaded the subway system and were planning to take over the world.

- The prosecutor did her best to *substantiate* the charge against the defendant, but it was an uphill job; she couldn't find a single witness willing to testify against him.

- Lawrence's entire scientific career is built on *unsubstantiated* theories; a case in point is his ten-year study of communication between rocks.

Substantial is a related word that means "of significant size, worth, or importance." You could say that by *substantiating* something, you make it more *substantial*.

superficial (soo pur FISH ul) *adj* on the surface only; shallow; not thorough

---

Mnemonic:

If you think you have a SUPER FACE, then you might be SUPERFICIAL, concerned only with the SURFACE of things.

- Tom had indeed been shot, but the wound was *superficial;* the bullet had merely creased the tip of his nose.

- The mechanic, who was in a hurry, gave my car what appeared to be a *superficial* tune-up. In fact, if he checked the oil, he did it without opening the hood.

A person who is *superficial* can be accused of *superficiality:*

- The *superficiality* of the editor's comments made us think that he hadn't really read the manuscript.

undermine (UN dur myne) *v*   to impair; to subvert; to weaken by excavating underneath

Mnemonics:

- MINES are UNDER the earth. You would WEAKEN a building by digging MINES underneath it.

- Land MINES UNDER my feet would WEAKEN me.

- The children's adamant refusal to learn French considerably *undermines* their teacher's efforts to teach it to them.

- The rushing waters of the flood had *undermined* the north end of the foundation, and the house was now leaning in that direction.

underscore (un dur SKOHR) *v*   to underline; to emphasize

Mnemonics:

- If you UNDERLINE important key points on the test, you will SCORE high.
- The UNDERSCORE key on your keyboard EMPHASIZES text.

- Heidi was so nervous about the exam that she ended up *underscoring* her entire textbook in yellow marker.
- "I hate you!" Ryan shouted. To *underscore* his point, he added, "I think you stink!"
- Harold's terrible hunger *underscores* the importance of remembering to eat.

Now are you ready for some practice exercises? Turn to the next page and put your vocabulary knowledge to the test. Try using mnemonic devices (either the ones discussed in this chapter or your own) to help you.

Chapter 5 Practice Exercises

Fill in the Blank

Choose the word that best completes the sentence. Answers can be found on page 137.

1. Xavier thought that throwing some scraps to the bear would _____ it, but instead the bear tore apart our campsite in search of more to eat.
   A) elucidate
   B) placate
   C) impugn
   D) denounce

2. Mei _____ her daughter for putting the cat in the washing machine.
   A) mediated
   B) revoked
   C) anthropomorphized
   D) denounced

3. David's salary was _____ his limited skills; he was paid nothing.
   A) as empirical as
   B) as explicit as
   C) indifferent to
   D) proportionate to

4. After several decades of peace, the little country grew _____ about defense and let its army slowly dwindle.
   A) nostalgic
   B) objective
   C) ominous
   D) complacent

5. None of us had enough money to undertake the project alone, so we had to depend on the _____ of our parents.
   A) pervasiveness
   B) resignation
   C) philanthropy
   D) substantiation

6. The court ruled that Ursula's superficial discussions with the Russian ambassador did not _____ treason.
   A) undermine
   B) impugn
   C) aver
   D) amount to

Word Relationships

Decide whether each pair of words below is roughly similar (S) in meaning, roughly opposite (O) in meaning, or unrelated (U) to each other. Answers can be found on page 138.

Set 1

1. credence	believability	_____
2. diction	dictum	_____
3. mercurial	changeable	_____
4. innocent	culpable	_____
5. indict	exculpate	_____
6. malediction	benediction	_____
7. nominate	renovate	_____
8. pseudonym	ignominy	_____
9. anonymous	autonomy	_____
10. nomenclature	innovation	_____

Set 2

1. novice   expert   _____
2. candor   equivocation   _____
3. nova   dignity   _____
4. indignant   disdainful   _____
5. veracity   verity   _____
6. eloquent   loquacious   _____
7. interlocutor   culprit   _____
8. ignorant   erudite   _____
9. amenable   amendable   _____
10. amity   antipathy   _____

Set 3

1. renovate   revive   _____
2. dignity   esteem   _____
3. indignation   complacence   _____
4. verdict   truth   _____
5. concurrent   anachronistic   _____
6. verisimilitude falsehood   _____
7. aver   deny   _____
8. anachronism   verity   _____
9. eloquent   well-spoken   _____
10. elocution   speech   _____

Set 4

1. anomaly   irregularity   _____
2. substandard   superior   _____
3. loquacious   quiet   _____
4. apprehensive   fearless   _____
5. brevity   candor   _____
6. conspicuous   transferred   _____
7. amorphous   cloudy   _____
8. deference   disrespect   _____
9. denounce   condemn   _____
10. lethargic   despondent   _____

Odd Man Out

Each row below consists of four words, three of which are related in meaning. Circle or underline the word that does not fit. Answers can be found on page 139.

Set 1

1. explicit	implicit	obvious	clear
2. indifferent	deferential	apathetic	uncaring
3. apt	inept	clumsy	incompetent
4. tempo	pace	rhythm	chronicle
5. nominal	amiable	amenable	friendly
6. lament	mourn	grieve	equate
7. malleable	bendable	nostalgic	polymorphous
8. mediate	negotiate	meditate	placate
9. subjective	objective	biased	prejudiced
10. anonymous	hidden	nominated	pseudonym

Set 2

1. culpable	guilty	innocent	blame-worthy
2. ambiguous	equivocal	vague	clear
3. apprehensive	brave	fearful	nervous
4. ambitious	amorous	amiable	amicable
5. luminous	luminescent	lucid	lackluster
6. intractable	intransigent	stubborn	placid
7. complacent	pugnacious	aggressive	pugilistic
8. extemporaneous	modern	contemporary	contemporaneous
9. chronic	acute	sharp	shrewd
10. undermine	underscore	highlight	emphasize

Chapter 5 Answer Key

Chapter 4 Review

1. Our **amiable** guide made us feel _welcome_ in what would otherwise have been a cold and forbidding museum.

2. The **credulous** housewife _believed_ that she had won a million dollars through an e-mail scam.

3. The accountant's _guilt; misconduct_ made him **culpable** in the tax-fraud case.

4. In **elocution** class, Brad learned _the art of speaking; how to speak well_.

5. Babies can mash food into their hair with **impunity**; no one _blames_ them.

6. The **intractable** child was _stubborn; defiant_ to his nursery school teacher.

7. Hubert's remarks were few but **lucid**: He _clarified_ the complicated issue with just a handful of well-chosen words.

8. The snow on the ground appeared eerily **luminous** at night; it seemed to _glow; shine with light_.

9. It would be easier to trust Charlotte if she had a reputation for being **veracious**—but she doesn't. In fact, she's been called a _liar_ many times before.

Fill in the Blank

1. **B** The word *but* indicates a change in direction within the sentence. The "bear tore apart our campsite" sounds negative, so you are looking for a positive word. Choices (C) and (D) contain negative roots, so the answer must be either (A) or (B). *Luc-* refers to light, and one would not make a bear "clear," so you are left with (B). *Plac-* means "calm."

2. **D** "Putting the cat in the washing machine" is definitely negative, so eliminate (A) and (C). To *revoke* means to take something back, so (D) is better: Mei condemned or criticized her daughter.

3. **D** David had "limited skills" and he was "paid nothing." So his salary was in harmony with, or *proportionate to,* his skills. Choice (D) is correct.

4. **D** The clue is "let its army slowly dwindle," which suggests that the country grew unconcerned with defense, suggesting that it was perhaps too comfortable, or *complacent.* The answer is (D).

5. **C** Notice the phrase "None of us had enough money to undertake the project alone." They had to rely on their parents' money. Choice (C) literally means "love of people," but it often implies a gift of money. The answer is (C).

6. **D** The clue in this sentence is "superficial." You may remember from earlier in this chapter that *superficial* means "shallow" or "meaningless." So, these kinds of discussions would not *amount to* treason. Choice (D) is the answer.

Word Relationships

Set 1

1. S
2. U
3. S
4. O
5. O
6. O
7. U
8. U
9. U
10. U

Set 2

1. O
2. O
3. U
4. S
5. S
6. U
7. U
8. O
9. U
10. O

Set 3

1. S
2. S
3. O
4. S
5. O
6. O
7. O
8. U
9. S
10. S

Set 4

1. S
2. O
3. O
4. O
5. U
6. U
7. S
8. O
9. S
10. S

Odd Man Out

Set 1

1. implicit
2. deferential
3. apt
4. chronicle
5. nominal
6. equate
7. nostalgic
8. meditate
9. objective
10. nominated

Set 2

1. innocent
2. clear
3. brave
4. ambitious
5. lackluster
6. placid
7. complacent
8. extemporaneous
9. chronic
10. undermine

Now It's Your Turn

CHAPTER 6

Create Your Own Mnemonics

Now It's Your Turn

Now that you've learned a number of words using our mnemonics, it's time to put your creativity to the test by coming up with some of your own. The following is a list of words and their definitions. Create your own special mnemonic for each one, remembering to visualize the definition of the word. If you're having trouble thinking of your own mnemonic, we've provided a picture clue for each word to help you out. (Otherwise, feel free to ignore the clues—you've got this!) Remember, mnemonics are effective when they are unique and unforgettable—the sillier, the better!

We recommend creating flashcards for these words and including your mnemonic for each word on the back of the card along with the definition. If you want to see our suggestions for mnemonics for the words in this chapter, see page 162.

ascertain (as ur TAYN) *v*   to determine with certainty; to find out definitely

- With a quick flick of his tongue, Wendell *ascertained* that the pie that had just landed on his face was indeed lemon meringue.

- The police tried to trace the phone call, but they were unable to *ascertain* the exact location of the caller.

- Larry believed his wife was seeing another man; the private detective *ascertained* that this was the case.

assimilate (uh SIM uh layt) *v* to take in; to absorb; to learn thoroughly

Mnemonic: _____

To *assimilate* an idea is to take it in as thoroughly, as though eating it. (Your body *assimilates* nutrients from the food you eat.) To *assimilate* knowledge is to absorb it, to let it soak in. People can be *assimilated,* too.

- Margaret didn't have any friends when she first went to the new school, but she was gradually *assimilated*—she became part of the new community. When she was chosen for the cheerleading squad, her *assimilation* was complete.

astute (uh STOOT) *adj*   shrewd; keen in judgment

Mnemonic: _____

- Morris was an *astute* judge of character; he was very good at seeing what people were really like despite what they pretended to be.
- Yael, who notices everything important and many things that other people don't see, is an *astute* observer.

asylum (uh SYE lum) *n*   refuge; a place of safety

Mnemonic: _____

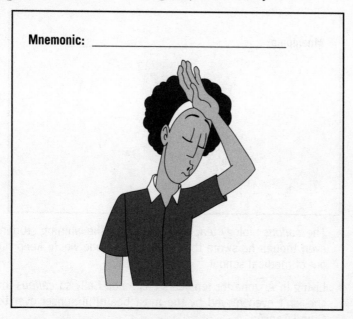

- "The woods are my *asylum*," Marjorie said. "I go there to escape the insanity of the world."

- The United States granted *asylum* to the political dissidents from a foreign country, thus permitting them to remain in the United States and not forcing them to return to their native country, where they certainly would have been imprisoned.

callous (KAL us) *adj*   insensitive; emotionally hardened

> **Mnemonic:** _____
>
>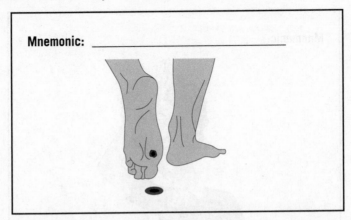

- The *callous* biology teacher gave a B to the whining student, even though he swore that such a low grade would keep him out of medical school.

- Living in Arizona for ten years has made Sally so *callous* that she isn't even moved by the most beautiful sunset over the Grand Canyon.

- A *callus* (KAL us) is a patch of thickened or roughened skin. A *callous* person is someone who has a metaphorical *callus* covering his or her emotions. (Notice the difference in spelling between *callous* and *callus*.)

arly didn't like answering

nd; isolated

d is *insula.* From it we get the words *penin-*
d"), *insulate* (*insulation* makes a house an
sular, among others.
e community had very little contact with the

nsular has *insularity.*
y of the little community was so complete that it
ble to buy a big-city newspaper there.

erudition (ER eh di shen) *n* impressive or extensive knowledge, usually achieved by studying and schooling; scholarly knowledge

Mnemonic: _____

- Mr. Fernicola's vast library was an indication of his *erudition.*

To be *erudite* is to possess *erudition.*

- The professor said such *erudite* things that none of us had the slightest idea of what he was saying.

- The *erudite* biologist was viewed by many of his colleagues as a likely winner of the Nobel Prize.

gaffe (gaf) *n*   a social blunder; an embarrassing mistake; a faux pas

Mnemonic: _____

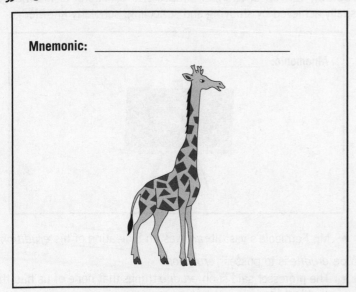

- In some cultures, burping after you eat is considered a sign that you liked the meal. In our culture, it's considered a *gaffe*.

- You commit a *gaffe* when you ask a man if he's wearing a toupee.

- Michael Kinsley defines a politician's *gaffe* as "when one inadvertently tells the truth."

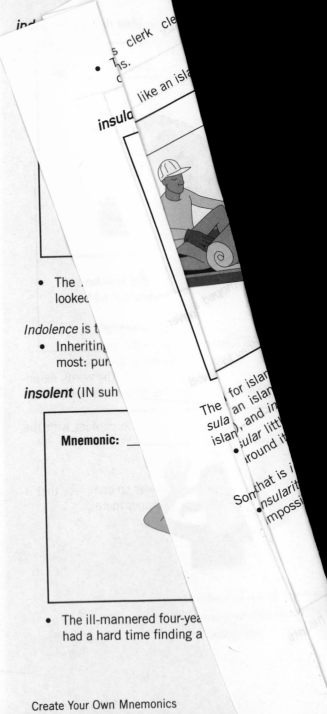

- The
  looked

Indolence is t

- Inheriting
  most: pur

insolent (IN suh

Mnemonic: ___

The for islan
an islan
sula , and *in
islan*
sular littl
around it

Som that is *i
nsularit
mpossi

- The ill-mannered four-yea
  had a hard time finding a

malinger (muh LING ger) *v*   to pretend to be sick to avoid doing work

Mnemonic: _____

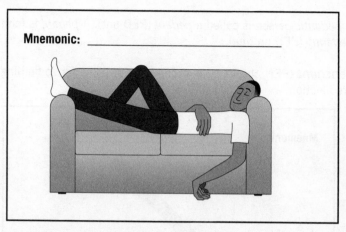

- Indolent Leon always *malingered* when it was his turn to clean up the house.

- Arthur is artful: He always manages to *malinger* before a big exam.

pedantic (puh DAN tik) *adj*   boringly scholarly or academic

Mnemonic: _____

- The discussion quickly turned *pedantic* as each participant tried to sound more learned than all the others.

- The professor's interpretation of the poem was *pedantic* and empty of genuine feeling.

A *pedantic* person is called a *pedant* (PED unt). A *pedant* is fond of *pedantry* (PED un tree).

penchant (PEN chunt) *n*   a strong taste or liking for something; a predilection

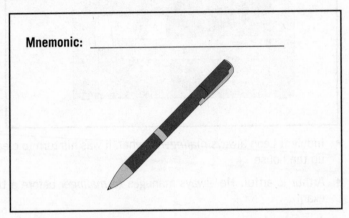

Mnemonic: _____

- Dogs have a *penchant* for chasing cats and mail carriers.

penitent (PEN uh tunt) *adj*   sorry; repentant; contrite

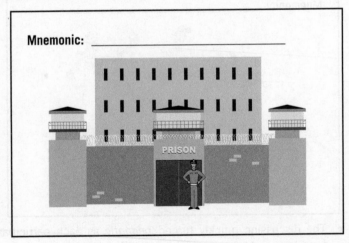

Mnemonic: _____

SAT Power Vocab

- Julie was *penitent* when Kanye explained how much pain she had caused him.
- The two boys tried to sound *penitent* at the police station, but they weren't really sorry that they had herded the sheep into Mr. Ingersoll's house. They were *impenitent*.

pragmatic (prag MAT ik) *adj*   practical; down-to-earth; based on experience rather than theory

Mnemonic: _____

A *pragmatic* person is one who deals with things as they are rather than as they might be or should be.

- Erecting a gigantic dome of gold over our house would have been the ideal solution to fix the leak in our roof, but the small size of our bank account forced us to be *pragmatic;* we patched the hole with a dab of tar instead.

Pragmatism (PRAG muh tiz um) is the belief or philosophy that the value or truth of something can be measured by its practical consequences.

proliferate (proh LIF uh rayt) *v*   to spread or grow rapidly

prolific (proh LIF ik) *adj*   abundantly productive; fruitful or fertile

Proliferate and *prolific* are very similar in meaning, so create one mnemonic for both:

Mnemonic: _____

proliferate
- Honeybees *proliferated* when we filled our yard with flowering plants.

- Coughs and colds *proliferate* when groups of children are cooped up together during the winter.

- The police didn't know what to make of the *proliferation* of counterfeit money in the north end of town.

prolific
- A *prolific* writer writes a lot of books. A *prolific* artist creates a lot of artwork.

- The old man had been extraordinarily *prolific;* he had thirty children and more than one hundred grandchildren.

reticent (RET uh sint) *adj* quiet; restrained; reluctant to speak, especially about oneself

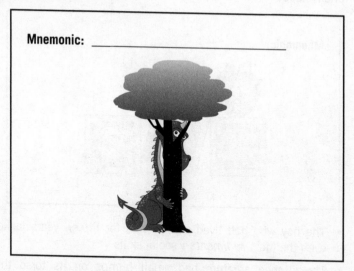

Mnemonic: _____

- Luther's natural *reticence* made him an ideal speaker: His speeches never lasted more than a few minutes.

- Kaynard was *reticent* on the subject of his accomplishments; he didn't like to talk about himself.

To be *reticent* is to be characterized by *reticence*.

rudimentary (roo duh MEN tuh ree) *adj* basic; crude; unformed or undeveloped

Mnemonic: _____

- The boy who had lived with wolves for fifteen years lacked even the most *rudimentary* social skills.
- The strange creature had small bumps on its torso that appeared to be *rudimentary* limbs.

sagacious (suh GAY shus) *adj* discerning; shrewd; keen in judgment; wise

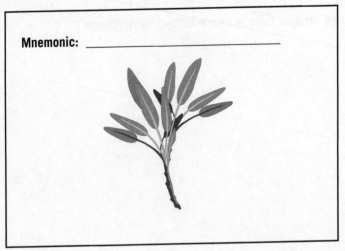

Mnemonic: _____

- Edgar's decision to move the chickens into the barn turned out to be *sagacious;* about an hour later, the hailstorm hit.

- The announcer's *sagacious* commentary made the baseball game seem vastly more profound than we had expected it to be.

To be *sagacious* is to have *sagacity* (suh GAS uh tee). A similar word is *sage,* which means wise, possessing wisdom derived from experience or learning.

- When we were contemplating starting our own popcorn business, we received some *sage* advice from a man who had lost all his money selling candied apples.

- The professor's critique, which comprised a few *sage* comments, sent me back to my dorm feeling pretty stupid.

Sage can also be a noun. A wise person, especially a wise old person, is often called a *sage.*

Bonus Exercise

Using your knowledge of roots and mnemonic skills, create your own definition and example sentence for the following word. You can compare your answers with ours on page 158.

PRESAGE [PRES ij] v

Definition: _____

_____

Sentence: _____

_____

specious (SPEE shus) *adj*   deceptively plausible or attractive

Mnemonic: _____

- The charlatan's *specious* theories about curing baldness with used tea bags charmed the studio audience but did not convince the experts, who believed that fresh tea bags were more effective.

- The river's beauty turned out to be *specious;* what had looked like churning rapids from a distance was, upon closer inspection, some sort of foamy industrial waste.

To be *specious* is to be characterized by *speciousness.*

Bonus Exercise Answer

Definition: *Presage* means to know (*sage*) something before (*pre-*) it happens; to foreshadow. It suggests an omen or warning sign.

Sentence: The team's devastating loss on homecoming weekend *presaged* the rest of the season; they finished last in the league.

tentative (TEN tuh tiv) *adj*   experimental; temporary; uncertain

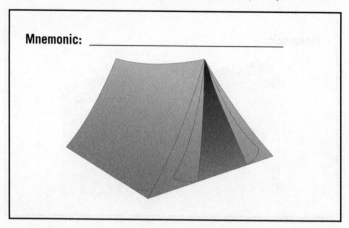

Mnemonic: _____

- George made a *tentative* effort to paint his house by himself; he slapped some paint on the front door and his clothes, tipped over the bucket, and called a professional.

- Our plans for the party are *tentative* at this point, but we are considering hiring a troupe of accordionists to play polkas while our guests are eating dessert.

- Hugo believed himself to be a great wit, but his big joke was rewarded by nothing more than a very *tentative* chuckle from his audience.

tenuous (TEN yoo us) *adj* flimsy; extremely thin

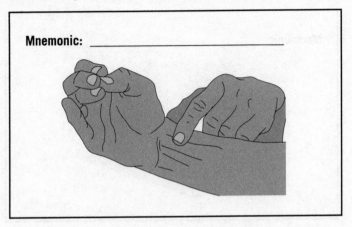

Mnemonic: _____

- The organization's financial situation has always been *tenuous;* the balance of the checking account is usually close to zero.

To *attenuate* is to make thin. *Extenuating* circumstances are those that lessen the magnitude of something, especially a crime.

- Cherrie admitted that she stole the snacks but claimed that there were *extenuating* circumstances: She had no money to buy food for her dog.

Chapter 6 Practice Exercises

SAT Quick Quiz

Here's your first SAT Quick Quiz! The passage below is similar to those you will see in longer passages on the SAT Reading section. Read the passage and answer the questions that follow. Answers can be found on page 163.

What the ordinary person generally means by imitation of a large subject—say a landscape—is a mirror copy much like a colored photograph: nature with its infinite mass of details
Line crowded into the picture, unsifted, unassimilated, and unarranged.
5 Even if it were possible to put in everything seen, it would not be art any more than copying a poem is creating poetry.

The painter uses nature not as a copybook but as a source of inspiration, selects such details as suits his or her purpose, and arranges them in a picture with a discriminating regard for
10 pictorial effect.

1

As used in line 4, "unassimilated" most nearly means

A) sorted.

B) distinct.

C) untouched.

D) discriminated against.

2

As used in line 9, "discriminating" most nearly means

A) prejudiced.

B) hostile.

C) selective.

D) artistic.

Chapter 6 Answer Key

Create Your Own Mnemonics

You can use the list below to compare your mnemonics with ours. Remember, these are just suggestions—there is no one correct answer!

ascertain: To make CERTAIN or be CERTAIN

assimilate: To make SIMILAR

astute: Good STUDENTS are ASTUTE.

asylum: You can breathe A SIGH of relief in a place of ASYLUM.

callous: The CALLUS on your foot is HARD and LACKS FEELING.

erudition: People who know a lot about ADDITION have ERUDITION.

gaffe: A GIRAFFE has an awkward or EMBARRASSING neck.

indolent: People who feel DULL are often INDOLENT.

insolent: INSOLENT sounds like/looks like INSULTING.

insular: An INSULAR place is INSULATED (ISOLATED) from everything else.

malinger: When you LINGER on the couch all day, you may be MALINGERing.

pedantic: The DANCE teacher is rather PEDANTIC. (Picture a STRICT dance teacher.)

penchant: My grandfather has a PENCHANT for nice PENS.

penitent: People in a PENITENTIARY are (or should be) PENITENT.

pragmatic: PRAGMATIC pianists know that PRACTICE makes perfect.

proliferate/prolific: LIFE GROWS and SPREADS.

reticent: If you are not READY for people (socially), you will be RETICENT.

rudimentary: RUDIMENTARY rhymes with ELEMENTARY.

sagacious: It is WISE to put SAGE in your turkey stuffing at Thanksgiving.

specious: The unicorn is a SPECIOUS SPECIES.

tentative: Putting up a TENT is a TENTATIVE job.

tenuous: Your TENDONS are TENUOUS.

SAT Quick Quiz

1. **C** To *assimilate* means "to make similar," so *unassimilated* is an adjective meaning something like "not included in the whole." In the sentence in question, the meaning closest to *unassimilated* in this context is (C).

2. **C** A person with a refined aesthetic sense is able to *discriminate* subtle differences where a less observant person would see nothing. Such a person is discriminating, and their tastes may be picky, or *selective*. Choice (C) is correct. (Note: Don't confuse *discriminating* with *discriminatory*, which is negative and often used to mean something like "prejudiced.")

Word Associations

Word Associations = Powerful Mnemonics

Let's face it: There are probably some words you have heard and used over and over throughout your life without ever knowing the real definitions of them. However, you may associate such words with certain images or ideas, even though you are unsure of the precise definition.

For instance, take a word like *kudos*. You may have heard this word often in the context of something like, "Kudos to everyone who helped plan this successful event." Or, perhaps you're familiar with the snack of the same name. Your associations with this word help you figure out and remember the meaning, which is praise or congratulations. Hidden within these word associations are powerful mnemonics.

This chapter contains a list of words you may have heard at some point in your life, whether in the classroom or from a book, TV show, website, or fun party conversation. Your job is to come up with associations you have with the word, predict its definition, and then take a stab at the actual definition. Try to remember what other words or ideas you may associate with them or think about what the word *sounds like*. If you can't predict the full definition of the word, determine whether the word has a positive or negative meaning. You can use the Word List at the end of the chapter if you don't know the actual definition of a word. There are also answers provided at the end of the chapter starting on page 178. And before you dive into the list, here's an example, using the same word discussed above:

Word	kudos
Word Association/ Sounds Like	*brand of granola bar;* "*Kudos on the award*"
Predicted Definition	*Not sure, but it must be something positive; they wouldn't name a candy bar after something bad.*
Actual Definition	*praise*

Chapter 7 Practice Exercises

Word Associations

You can check your answers against ours on page 178.

ABSTRUSE (ab STROOS)

Word Association/Sounds Like: _____

Predicted Definition: _____

Actual Definition: _____

AFFRONT (uh FRUNT)

Word Association/Sounds Like: _____

Predicted Definition: _____

Actual Definition: _____

ALLEVIATE (uh LEE vee ayt)

Word Association/Sounds Like: _____

Predicted Definition: _____

Actual Definition: _____

ALLOCATE (AL uh kayt)

Word Association/Sounds Like: _____

Predicted Definition: _____

Actual Definition: _____

BLUSTER (BLUS tur)

Word Association/Sounds Like: _____

Predicted Definition: _____

Actual Definition: _____

BOMBAST (BAHM bast)

Word Association/Sounds Like: _____

Predicted Definition: _____

Actual Definition: _____

BRAWN (brawn)

Word Association/Sounds Like: _____

Predicted Definition: _____

Actual Definition: _____

CASTIGATE (KAS tuh gayt)

Word Association/Sounds Like: _____

Predicted Definition: _____

Actual Definition: _____

CEREBRAL (suh REE brul)

Word Association/Sounds Like: _____

Predicted Definition: _____

Actual Definition: _____

CONTIGUOUS (kun TIG yoo us)

Word Association/Sounds Like: _____

Predicted Definition: _____

Actual Definition: _____

CORRUGATED (KOHR uh gay tud)

Word Association/Sounds Like: _____

Predicted Definition: _____

Actual Definition: _____

COSMOPOLITAN (kahz muh PAHL uh tun)

Word Association/Sounds Like: _____

Predicted Definition: _____

Actual Definition: _____

EPITOME (i PIT uh mee)

Word Association/Sounds Like: _____

Predicted Definition: _____

Actual Definition: _____

EXORBITANT (ig ZOHR buh tent)

Word Association/Sounds Like: _____

Predicted Definition: _____

Actual Definition: _____

EXPATRIATE (eks PAY tree ayt)

Word Association/Sounds Like: _____

Predicted Definition: _____

Actual Definition: _____

EXPEDIENT (ik SPEE dee ent)

Word Association/Sounds Like: _____

Predicted Definition: _____

Actual Definition: _____

EXPEDITE (EK spi dyte)

Word Association/Sounds Like: _____

Predicted Definition: _____

Actual Definition: _____

FALLACY (FAL uh see)

Word Association/Sounds Like: _____

Predicted Definition: _____

Actual Definition: _____

FISCAL (FIS kul)

Word Association/Sounds Like: _____

Predicted Definition: _____

Actual Definition: _____

FLAGRANT (FLAY grunt)

Word Association/Sounds Like: _____

Predicted Definition: _____

Actual Definition: _____

FLAUNT (flawnt)

Word Association/Sounds Like: _____

Predicted Definition: _____

Actual Definition: _____

FLEDGLING (FLEJ ling) (adj.)

Word Association/Sounds Like: _____

Predicted Definition: _____

Actual Definition: _____

FLIPPANT (FLIP unt)

Word Association/Sounds Like: _____

Predicted Definition: _____

Actual Definition: _____

LAUD (lawd)

Word Association/Sounds Like: _____

Predicted Definition: _____

Actual Definition: _____

LAVISH (LAV ish)

Word Association/Sounds Like: _____

Predicted Definition: _____

Actual Definition: _____

MERCENARY (MUR suh ner ee)

Word Association/Sounds Like: _____

Predicted Definition: _____

Actual Definition: _____

ORTHODOX (OR thuh dahks)

Word Association/Sounds Like: _____

Predicted Definition: _____

Actual Definition: _____

OSCILLATE (AHS uh layt)

Word Association/Sounds Like: _____

Predicted Definition: _____

Actual Definition: _____

PALLIATIVE (PAL ee ah tiv)

Word Association/Sounds Like: _____

Predicted Definition: _____

Actual Definition: _____

PARTISAN (PAHR tuh zun)

Word Association/Sounds Like: _____

Predicted Definition: _____

Actual Definition: _____

RHETORIC (RET ur ik)

Word Association/Sounds Like: _____

Predicted Definition: _____

Actual Definition: _____

SQUANDER (SKWAHN dur)

Word Association/Sounds Like: _____

Predicted Definition: _____

Actual Definition: _____

TANGENTIAL (tan JEN shul)

Word Association/Sounds Like: _____

Predicted Definition: _____

Actual Definition: _____

VESTIGE (VES tij)

Word Association/Sounds Like: _____

Predicted Definition: _____

Actual Definition: _____

VEX (veks)

Word Association/Sounds Like: _____

Predicted Definition: _____

Actual Definition: _____

VIE (vye)

Word Association/Sounds Like: _____

Predicted Definition: _____

Actual Definition: _____

VIGILANT (VIJ uh lunt)

Word Association/Sounds Like: _____

Predicted Definition: _____

Actual Definition: _____

Words in Context

Read each passage and determine the meaning of the words in bold based on the context of the paragraph. Answers can be found on page 187.

If a painting is an unsifted mass of objects, it fails at the very point where art begins, the point that marks the difference between art and imitation. One of the **pathetic fallacies** of art is that realism of fact creates realism of effect, that increasing the facts of nature in a picture or sculpture increases the "feeling of Nature" in it. On the contrary, such techniques decrease the sensation because fullness of fact leaves too little to the imagination.

1. **pathetic** _____

_____

2. **fallacy** _____

_____

Chapter 7 Answer Key

Word Associations

ABSTRUSE

Word Association/Sounds Like:	abstract, obtuse
Predicted Definition:	weird; hard to figure out
Actual Definition:	hard to understand

AFFRONT

Word Association/Sounds Like:	getting in "front"
Predicted Definition:	in front of
Actual Definition:	insult; "in your face"

ALLEVIATE

Word Association/Sounds Like:	relieve; leave
Predicted Definition:	painkiller
Actual Definition:	to relieve

ALLOCATE

Word Association/Sounds Like:	locate; "allocate money"
Predicted Definition:	to find or put aside
Actual Definition:	to distribute; to assign

BLUSTER

Word Association/Sounds Like:	blustery weather
Predicted Definition:	negative; lousy; windy
Actual Definition:	to be loud or aggressive

BOMBAST

Word Association/Sounds Like:	bomb
Predicted Definition:	explosive; big; major event
Actual Definition:	pompous speech

BRAWNY

Word Association/Sounds Like:	"brains, not brawn"
Predicted Definition:	big, powerful, not brainy
Actual Definition:	having muscles, strength

CASTIGATE

Word Association/Sounds Like:	cast down, cast away
Predicted Definition:	something negative
Actual Definition:	criticize severely

CEREBRAL

Word Association/Sounds Like: cerebellum, cerebrum, the brain

Predicted Definition: smart

Actual Definition: brainy

CONTIGUOUS

Word Association/Sounds Like: continuous; "48 contiguous United States"

Predicted Definition: ongoing; touching

Actual Definition: side by side

CORRUGATED

Word Association/Sounds Like: corrugated cardboard

Predicted Definition: thick, ridgy

Actual Definition: shaped with folds or waves

COSMOPOLITAN

Word Association/Sounds Like: metropolitan

Predicted Definition: cool, modern

Actual Definition: sophisticated

EPITOME

Word Association/Sounds Like: "the epitome of greatness"

Predicted Definition: ultimate example

Actual Definition: the perfect example of something

EXORBITANT

Word Association/Sounds Like: prices; "out of orbit"

Predicted Definition: high; "out there"

Actual Definition: excessive

EXPATRIATE

Word Association/Sounds Like: "out of" + patriot

Predicted Definition: no longer a patriot

Actual Definition: to move away from one's native land

EXPEDIENT

Word Association/Sounds Like: speed, speedy

Predicted Definition: travel; fast; must be positive

Actual Definition: providing an immediate advantage

EXPEDITE

Word Association/Sounds Like: "in order to expedite the handling of your call," expedited shipping, sounds like **expedient**

Predicted Definition: make faster

Actual Definition: to speed up

FALLACY

Word Association/Sounds Like: false

Predicted Definition: false

Actual Definition: a false idea

FISCAL

Word Association/Sounds Like: "fiscal responsibility"; politics

Predicted Definition: having to do with politics or budgets

Actual Definition: pertaining to financial matters

FLAGRANT

Word Association/Sounds Like: "flagrant foul" (basketball)

Predicted Definition: bad; out of line

Actual Definition: glaringly bad

FLAUNT

Word Association/Sounds Like:	"if you've got it, flaunt it"; flaunting your wealth
Predicted Definition:	to show off
Actual Definition:	to show off

FLEDGLING

Word Association/Sounds Like:	a baby bird
Predicted Definition:	something young or weak
Actual Definition:	inexperienced; immature

FLIPPANT

Word Association/Sounds Like:	"flip out"
Predicted Definition:	crazy; out of control
Actual Definition:	frivolously disrespectful

LAUD

Word Association/Sounds Like:	applaud
Predicted Definition:	to applaud; to praise
Actual Definition:	praise

LAVISH

Word Association/Sounds Like: "living a lavish lifestyle"

Predicted Definition: wealthy; over-the-top

Actual Definition: to spend freely

MERCENARY

Word Association/Sounds Like: "mercenary soldiers"

Predicted Definition: fighting

Actual Definition: fighting or doing anything for money

ORTHODOX

Word Association/Sounds Like: religion

Predicted Definition: religious

Actual Definition: adhering to established principles

OSCILLATE

Word Association/Sounds Like: oscillating fan

Predicted Definition: spinning; windy; fast

Actual Definition: to swing back and forth

             SAT Power Vocab

PALLIATIVE

Word Association/Sounds Like:	"palliative medicine/care"
Predicted Definition:	helpful; healthy
Actual Definition:	relieving symptoms without effecting a cure

PARTISAN

Word Association/Sounds Like:	"partisan politics," "bipartisan support," parties, parts
Predicted Definition:	political friendship
Actual Definition:	one who supports a particular person or idea

RHETORIC

Word Association/Sounds Like:	"politicians are full of rhetoric," rhetorical skills, rhetorical question
Predicted Definition:	lies; writing, speaking, asking
Actual Definition:	the art of speaking or writing; can be inflated

SQUANDER

Word Association/Sounds Like:	"you shouldn't squander your money"
Predicted Definition:	to waste or spend
Actual Definition:	to waste

Word Associations

TANGENTIAL

Word Association/Sounds Like: tangent lines (geometry), "going off on tangents"

Predicted Definition: touching; rambling

Actual Definition: irrelevant, off-topic

VESTIGE

Word Association/Sounds Like: "the last vestiges of _____"

Predicted Definition: remains, remnants

Actual Definition: a remaining bit of something

VEX

Word Association/Sounds Like: hex; sounds bad

Predicted Definition: something negative

Actual Definition: to annoy

VIE

Word Association/Sounds Like: "to vie for _____"

Predicted Definition: to compete

Actual Definition: to compete

SAT Power Vocab

VIGILANT

Word Association/Sounds Like:	candlelight vigil; vigilante
Predicted Definition:	an event; attention; revenge
Actual Definition:	constantly alert; watchful

Words in Context
1. **pathetic:** pitiable
2. **fallacy:** a false idea

Chapter 7 Word List

ABSTRUSE (ab STROOS) *adj*   hard to understand
- The professor's article, on the "meaning of meaning," was *abstruse*. Michael couldn't even pronounce the words in it.
- Nuclear physics is a subject that is too *abstruse* for most people.

AFFRONT (uh FRUNT) *n*   insult; a deliberate act of disrespect
- Jim's dreadful score on the back nine was an *affront* to the ancient game of golf.
- Amanda thought she was paying Liz a compliment when she said that she liked her new hair color, but Liz took it as an *affront* because she was upset about the greenish spots the hair stylist couldn't cover.

Affront can also be a verb.
- Laura *affronted* me by continually sticking out her tongue as I addressed the class.

Rude and disrespectful behavior can be described as *effrontery* (i FRUN tuh ree).

ALLEVIATE (uh LEE vee ayt) *v*   to relieve, usually temporarily or incompletely; to make bearable; to lessen
- Visiting the charming pet cemetery *alleviated* the woman's grief over the death of her canary.
- Aspirin *alleviates* headache pain. When your headache comes back, take some more aspirin.

ALLOCATE (AL uh kayt) *v*   to distribute; to assign; to allot
- The event had been a big failure, and David, Aaliyah, and Jan spent several hours attempting to *allocate* the blame. In the end, they decided it had all been Jan's fault.
- The office manager had *allocated* just seven paper clips for our entire department.

BLUSTER (BLUS tur) *v*   to roar; to be loud; to be tumultuous
- The cold winter wind *blustered* all day long, rattling the windows and chilling everyone to the bone.

A day during which the wind *blusters* would be a *blustery* (BLUS tur ee) day.
- The golfers happily blamed all their bad shots on the *blustery* weather.

Bluster can also be a noun.
- Sadie was so used to her mother's angry shouting that she was able to tune out the *bluster* and get along with her work.

BOMBAST (BAHM bast) *n* pompous or pretentious speech or writing
- If you stripped away the *bombast* from the candidate's campaign speeches, you would find nothing but misconceptions and lies.

- The magazine writer resorted to *bombast* whenever his deadline was looming; thoughtful opinions required time and reflection, but he could become pompous almost as rapidly as he could type.

The adjective is *bombastic* (bahm BAS tik).

BRAWN (brawn) *n*   big muscles; great strength
- All the other boys in the class thought it extremely unfair that Sean had both brains and *brawn*.

- The old engine didn't have the *brawn* to propel the tractor up the side of the steep hill.

To be *brawny* (BRAW nee) is to be muscular.
- The members of the football team were so *brawny* that each one needed two seats on the airplane in order to sit comfortably.

CASTIGATE (KAS tuh gayt) *v* to criticize severely; to chastise
- Jose's mother-in-law *castigated* him for forgetting to pick her up at the airport.

CEREBRAL (suh REE brul) *adj* brainy; intellectually refined
Your *cerebrum* is the biggest part of your brain. To be *cerebral* is to do and care about things that really smart people do and care about.
- A *cerebral* discussion is one that is filled with big words and concerns abstruse matters that ordinary people can't understand.
- Sebastian was too *cerebral* to be a baseball announcer; he kept talking about the existentialism of the outfield.

CONTIGUOUS (kun TIG yoo us) *adj* side by side; adjoining
- Two countries that share a border are *contiguous*, as are two events that happened one right after the other.
- If two countries are *contiguous*, the territory they cover is continuous. That is, it spreads or continues across both countries without any interruption.

CORRUGATED (KOHR uh gay tud) *adj* shaped with folds or waves
- *Corrugated* sheet metal is sheet metal that has been shaped so that it has ridges and valleys, like a ridged potato chip.
- Corduroy pants might be called *corrugated*.
- Much of the paperboard used in making cardboard cartons is *corrugated*.

COSMOPOLITAN (kahz muh PAHL uh tun) *adj* at home in many places or situations; internationally sophisticated
- Marcello's tastes are *cosmopolitan* when it comes to cuisine; he eats only the finest French foods.
- A truly *cosmopolitan* traveler never feels like a foreigner in any country.
- New York City is very *cosmopolitan*; you can hear nearly every language spoken there.

EPITOME (i PIT uh mee) *n* a brief summary that captures the meaning of the whole; the perfect example of something; a paradigm
- The first paragraph of the new novel is an *epitome* of the entire book; you can read it and understand what the author is trying to get across. It *epitomizes* the entire work.
- Luke's freshman year was the *epitome* of a college experience; he made friends, joined a fraternity, and ate too much pizza.
- Eating corn dogs and drinking root beer is the *epitome* of the good life, as far as Wilson is concerned.

EXORBITANT (ig ZOHR buh tent) *adj* excessively costly; excessive
This word literally means "out of orbit."
- Prices are *exorbitant* when they get sky-high.
- Meals at the new restaurant were *exorbitant*; a garden salad cost seventy-five dollars.
- The Better Business Bureau cited the discount electronic store for putting an *exorbitant* markup on portable tape recorders.

EXPATRIATE (eks PAY tree ayt) *v* to throw (someone) out of his or her native land; to move away from one's native land; to emigrate
- The rebels were *expatriated* by the nervous general, who feared that they would cause trouble if they were allowed to remain in the country.
- Hugo was fed up with his native country, so he *expatriated* to America. In doing so, Hugo became an *expatriate* (eks PAY tree ut).

To *repatriate* (ree PAY tree ayt) is to return to one's native citizenship, that is, to become a *repatriate* (ree PAY tree it).

EXPEDIENT (ik SPEE dee ent) *adj* providing an immediate advantage; serving one's immediate self-interest; practical
- Since the basement had nearly filled with water, the plumber felt it would be *expedient* to clear out the drain.
- The candidate's position in favor of higher pay for teachers was an *expedient* one adopted for the national teachers' convention but abandoned shortly afterward.

Expedient can also be used as a noun for something *expedient.*

- The car repairman did not have his tool kit handy, so he used chewing gum as an *expedient* to patch a hole.

The noun *expedience* or *expediency* also refers to practicality or being especially suited to a particular goal.

EXPEDITE (EK spi dyte) *v*   to speed up or ease the progress of

- The post office *expedited* mail delivery by hiring more letter carriers.

- The lawyer *expedited* the progress of our case through the courts by bribing a few judges.

- Our wait for a table was *expedited* by a waiter who mistook Angela for a movie star.

FALLACY (FAL uh see) *n*   a false notion or belief; a misconception

- Peter clung to the *fallacy* that he was a brilliant writer, despite the fact that everything he had ever written had been rejected by every publisher to whom he had sent it.

- That electricity is a liquid was but one of the many *fallacies* spread by the incompetent science teacher.

The adjective is *fallacious* (fuh LAY shus).

FISCAL (FIS kul) *adj*   pertaining to financial matters; monetary

- Having no sense of *fiscal* responsibility, he was happy to waste his salary on a life-size plastic flamingo with diamond eyes.

- A *fiscal* year is any twelve-month period established for accounting purposes.

- Scrooge Enterprises begins its *fiscal* year on December 25 to make sure that no one takes Christmas Day off.

FLAGRANT (FLAY grunt) *adj*   glaringly bad; notorious; scandalous

- An example of a *flagrant* theft would be stealing a car from the parking lot of a police station.

- A *flagrant* spelling error is a very noticeable one.

Don't confuse *flagrant* with *blatant,* which means "obvious."

FLAUNT (flawnt) *v*   to show off; to display ostentatiously
- The brand-new millionaire annoyed all his friends by driving around his old neighborhood to *flaunt* his new, expensive car.
- Colleen *flaunted* her engagement ring, shoving it in the face of almost anyone who came near her.

This word is very often confused with *flout,* which means to openly disregard or break a rule or law.

FLEDGLING (FLEJ ling) *adj*   inexperienced or immature
- A *fledgling* bird is one still too young to fly; once its wing feathers have grown in, it is said to be *fledged.*
- Lucy was still a *fledgling* caterer when her deviled eggs gave the whole party food poisoning.

Full-fledged means complete or full-grown.
- Now that Lucy is a *full-fledged* gourmet chef, her deviled eggs poison only a couple of people annually.

FLIPPANT (FLIP unt) *adj*   frivolously disrespectful; saucy; pert; flip
- I like to make *flippant* remarks in church to see how many old ladies will turn around and glare at me.

The act or state of being *flippant* is *flippancy* (FLIP un see).
- The *flippancy* of the second graders was almost more than the substitute teacher could stand.

Flip is another form of the word that is in common usage.

LAUD (lawd) *v*   to praise; to applaud; to extol; to celebrate
- The bank manager *lauded* the hero who trapped the escaping robber. The local newspaper published a *laudatory* editorial on this intrepid individual.

Laudatory means "praising," and *laudable* means "praiseworthy."
- Giving several million dollars to charity is a *laudable* act of philanthropy.

LAVISH (LAV ish) *v* to spend freely or bestow generously; to squander

- My father *lavishes* so many birthday presents on his relatives that they panic when it's time for them to give him something in return.

- City Hall has *lavished* money on the street-cleaning program, but our streets are dirtier than ever.

Lavish is also an adjective.

- Don't you think Miss Woodstone is a little too *lavish* with her praise? She slathers so much positive reinforcement on her students that they can't take her seriously at all.

MERCENARY (MUR suh ner ee) *n* a hired soldier; someone who will do anything for money

- If an army can't find enough volunteers or draftees, it will sometimes hire *mercenaries.* The magazine *Soldier of Fortune* is aimed at *mercenaries* and would-be *mercenaries;* it even runs classified advertisements by soldiers looking for someone to fight.

You don't have to be a soldier to be a *mercenary.* Someone who does something strictly for the money is often called a *mercenary.*

- Our business contains a few dedicated workers and many, many *mercenaries* who want to make a quick buck and then get out.

Mercenary can also be used as an adjective.

- Larry's motives in writing the screenplay for the trashy movie were strictly *mercenary*—he needed the money.

ORTHODOX (OR thuh dahks) *adj* conventional; adhering to established principles or doctrines, especially in religion; by the book

- The doctor's treatment for Lou's cold was entirely *orthodox:* plenty of liquids, aspirin, and rest.

- Austin's views were *orthodox;* there was nothing shocking about any of them.

The body of what is *orthodox* is called *orthodoxy.*
- The teacher's lectures were characterized by strict adherence to *orthodoxy.*

To be unconventional is to be *unorthodox.*
- "Swiss cheese" is an *unorthodox* explanation for the composition of the moon.

OSCILLATE (AHS uh layt) *v* to swing back and forth; to pulsate; to waver or vacillate between beliefs or ideas
- We watched the hypnotist's pendulum *oscillate* before our eyes, and soon we became sleepy.
- Mrs. Johnson can't make up her mind how to raise her children; she *oscillates* between strictness and laxity depending on what kind of mood she's in.

PALLIATE (PAL ee ayt) *v* to relieve or alleviate something without getting rid of the problem; to assuage; to mitigate
- You take aspirin in the hope that it will *palliate* your headache.
- Aspirin is a *palliative* (PAL yuh tiv).

PARTISAN (PAHR tuh zun) *n* one who supports a particular person, cause, or idea
- Henry's plan to give himself the award had no *partisan* except himself.
- I am the *partisan* of any candidate who promises not to make promises.
- The mountain village was attacked by *partisans* of the rebel chieftain.

Partisan can also be used as an adjective meaning "biased," as in *partisan politics.*
- An issue that everyone agrees on regardless of the party he or she belongs to is a *nonpartisan* issue.

Bipartisan means supported by two (bi) parties.
- Both the Republican and Democratic senators voted to give themselves a raise. The motion had *bipartisan* support.

RHETORIC (RET ur ik) *n*   the art of formal speaking or writing; inflated discourse
- A talented public speaker might be said to be skilled in *rhetoric*.

Rhetoric is often used in a pejorative sense to describe speaking or writing that is skillfully executed but insincere or devoid of meaning.
- The political candidate's speech that was long on drama and promises but short on genuine substance was dismissed as mere *rhetoric*.

SQUANDER (SKWAHN dur) *v*   to waste
- Jerry failed to husband his inheritance; instead, he *squandered* it on trips to Las Vegas.

TANGENTIAL (tan JEN shul) *adj*   only superficially related to the matter at hand; not especially relevant; peripheral
- The vice president's speech bore only a *tangential* relationship to the topic that had been announced.
- Stuart's connection with our organization is *tangential;* he once made a phone call from the lobby of our building, but he never worked here.
- When a writer or speaker "goes off on a *tangent*," he or she is making a digression or straying from the original topic.

VESTIGE (VES tij) *n*   a remaining bit of something; a last trace
- An old uniform and a tattered scrapbook were the only *vestiges* of the old man's career as a professional athlete.
- Your appendix is a *vestige:* It used to have a function, but now this organ does nothing.

The adjective form of *vestige* is *vestigial* (vuh STIJ ee ul).

- The appendix is referred to as a *vestigial* organ. It is still in our bodies, although it no longer has a function. It is a mere *vestige* of some function our digestive systems no longer perform.

VEX (veks) *v* to annoy; to pester; to confuse

- Margaret *vexed* me by poking me with a long, sharp stick.

The act of *vexing,* or the state of being *vexed,* is *vexation.* A *vexed* issue is one that is troubling or puzzling.

- Stuck at the bottom of a deep well, I found my situation extremely *vexing.*

VIE (vye) *v* to compete; to contest; to struggle

- Sheryl *vied* with her best friend for a promotion.

- The two advertising agencies *vied* fiercely for the Lax-Me-Up account, which was worth $100 million a year in billings.

VIGILANT (VIJ uh lunt) *adj* constantly alert; watchful; wary

- Miss Grimble is *vigilant* against grammatical errors; when she spots a misplaced modifier, she pounces like a tiger.

- Dad *vigilantly* guarded the door of the living room to keep the children from seeing the Easter Bunny at work.

To be *vigilant* is to exhibit *vigilance* (VIJ uh luns).

- Distracted by the loud noise in the hallway, the guard let his *vigilance* slip for a moment, and the prisoner quickly escaped.

Vigil is a related word that refers to a period of staying awake or peacefully protesting, as if *vigilantly* standing watch.

PART III

Practice, Practice, Practice

CHAPTER 8

New Words

Using the Knowledge You've Gained So Far

Congratulations—you're about two-thirds of the way done with this book! If you've been using it diligently, then you now know an abundance of new words. And it wasn't that painful, was it?

This chapter offers a change of pace by testing you on what you've learned thus far, allowing you to gauge how well you've absorbed the material.

The New Words Drill below may contain some words you do not know, and some you may never have even seen before—and that's okay! Do your best, and then check your answers using the chapter Word List on page 206 or the answer key on page 226.

New Words Drill

1. What does it mean to say that the North Pole and South Pole are **antipodal**?

   _____

2. If a thesis is an idea, what is its **antithesis**?

   _____

3. An **autocrat** is a tyrant or dictator. How does the root *auto-* relate to this meaning?

   _____

4. Is **contraband** positive or negative? Why?

   _____

5. The two negotiators reached a **contretemps**. Is this positive or negative? Why?

   _____

6. What does it mean to perform a task **autonomously**?

_____

7. If *rehabilitate* means to "restore to good health," what does it mean to **debilitate**?

_____

8. If *bunk* is nonsense, what does it mean to **debunk** an argument?

_____

9. What does it mean if a machine is **defunct**?

_____

10. If the verb *regenerate* means "to replace or revitalize," what is a **degenerate** (adj.) person?

_____

11. Is a **dejected** person happy or sad?

_____

12. If *deplete* means "to use up," what does the adjective **replete** mean?

_____

13. Is a **magnanimous** person generous or stingy?

_____

14. If you live a **peripatetic** lifestyle, do you travel a lot or stay at home?

_____

15. The word **posterity** refers to future generations of people. What root is helpful in learning this word?

_____

16. Does **posthumously** mean "before death" or "after death"?

_____

17. Is a **malapropism** a proper or improper use of a word?

_____

18. What is the opposite of a **malignant** tumor?

_____

19. Your **vocation** is your career. How does the root *voc-* relate to this word?

_____

20. Which root is most relevant to the word **anthology**? *Anthro-* or *log-*?

_____

21. Are **disparate** groups similar or dissimilar?

_____

22. **Debase, decry, defame, defile, degrade, deplore,** and **deride** are all virtually identical in meaning. They are things you can do to a person or idea. Use your knowledge of *de-* to create a definition for these words.

_____

23. What does it mean to be **enamored** with something? Which root helps you determine this meaning?

_____

24. The words **impugn** and **impunity** have nearly opposite meanings even though they sound similar. What's different about the spellings of these words?

_____

25. Does **exonerate** mean to find an accused person guilty or innocent? What root did you use to determine this?

_____

26. Is **exculpate** more similar to or opposite of **exonerate**?

_____

Now use the following word list to go back and check your answers to the previous questions. If you still aren't sure, you can check the answer key at the end of the chapter. Be sure to complete the exercises starting on page 214. These are intended to help you hone your skills and expand your word knowledge.

Chapter 8 Word List

ANTHOLOGY (an THAHL uh jee) *n*   a collection, especially of literary works
- To *anthologize* (an THAHL uh jyze) a group of literary works or other objects is to collect them into an *anthology.*
    - The *Norton Anthology of English Literature* is a collection of important works by English writers.
    - The chief executive officer of the big company thought so highly of himself that he privately published an *anthology* of his sayings.
    - Mr. Bailey, a terrible hypochondriac, was a walking *anthology* of symptoms.

ANTIPODAL (an TIP ud ul) *adj*   situated on opposite sides of the Earth; exactly opposite
- The north and south poles are literally *antipodal*; that is, they are exactly opposite each other on the globe.

The noun is *antipodes* (an TIP uh deez).
- There is a group of islands near New Zealand called the Antipodes (an TIP uh deez). The islands were named by European explorers who believed they had traveled just about as far away from their home as they possibly could.

Antipodal can also be used to describe opposites that have nothing to do with geography.
- John and Mary held *antipodal* positions on the subject of working. Mary was for it, and John was against it.

ANTITHESIS (an TITH uh sis) *n*   the direct opposite
- Erin is the *antithesis* of Aaron: Erin is bright and beautiful; Aaron is dull and plain.

AUTOCRATIC (aw tuh KRAT ik) *adj*   ruling with absolute authority; extremely bossy
- The ruthless dictator's *autocratic* reign ended when the rebels blew up his palace with plastic explosives.

- A two-year-old can be very *autocratic*—he wants what he wants when he wants it.

- No one at our office liked the *autocratic* manager. He always insisted on having his own way, and he never let anyone make a decision without consulting him.

- An *autocrat* is an absolute ruler. *Autocracy* (aw TAHK ruh see), a system of government headed by an *autocrat,* is not democratic—the people don't get a say.

AUTONOMOUS (aw TAHN uh mus) *adj*   acting independently
- The law firm's West Coast office was quite *autonomous;* it never asked the East Coast office for permission before it did anything.

- An *autonomous* nation is one that is independent—it governs itself. It is said to have *autonomy.*

- To act *autonomously* is to act on your own authority. If something happens *autonomously,* it happens all by itself.

CONTRABAND (KAHN truh band) *n*   smuggled goods
- The military police looked for *contraband* in the luggage of the returning soldiers, and they found plenty of it, including captured enemy weapons and illegal drugs.

- The head of the dormitory classified all candy as *contraband* and then went from room to room confiscating it so that he could eat it himself.

CONTRETEMPS (KAHN truh tahn) *n*   an embarrassing occurrence; a mishap
- Newell lost his job over a little *contretemps* involving an office party, the photocopier, and his rear end.

DEBASE (di BAYS) *v*   to lower in quality or value; to degrade
- To deprive a single person of his or her constitutional rights *debases* the liberty of us all.

- The high school teacher's reputation as a great educator was *debased* when it was discovered that his students' test scores dropped by five points after they utilized his test-taking strategies.

The noun is *debasement.*

DEBILITATE (di BIL uh tayt) *v*   to weaken; to cripple
- The football player's career was ended by a *debilitating* injury to his knee.
- To become *debilitated* is to suffer a *debility*, which is the opposite of an *ability*.
- A surgeon who becomes *debilitated* is one who has lost the ability to operate on the *debilities* of other people.

DEBUNK (di BUNK) *v*   to expose the nonsense of
- The reporter's careful exposé *debunked* the company's claim that it had not been dumping radioactive waste into the Hudson River.
- Paul's reputation as a philanthropist was a towering lie just waiting to be *debunked*.

Bunk, by the way, is nonsense or meaningless talk.

DECRY (di KRY) *v*   to put down; to denounce
- The newspaper editorial *decried* efforts by the police chief to root out corruption in the police department, saying that the chief was himself corrupt and could not be trusted.
- The environmental organization quickly issued a report *decrying* the large mining company's plan to reduce the entire mountain to rubble in its search for uranium.

DEFAME (di FAYM) *v*   to libel or slander; to ruin the good name of
To *defame* someone is to make accusations that harm the person's reputation.
- The local businessman accused the newspaper of *defaming* him by publishing an article that said his company was poorly managed.

To *defame* is to take away fame, to take away a good name. To suffer such a loss of reputation is to suffer *defamation*.
- The businessman who believed he had been *defamed* by the newspaper sued the paper's publisher for *defamation*.

DEFILE (di FYLE) *v* to make filthy or foul; to desecrate

- The snowy field was so beautiful that I hated to *defile* it by driving across it.

- In the night, vandals *defiled* the painting behind the altar, covering it with spray paint.

DEFUNCT (di FUNKT) *adj* no longer in effect; no longer in existence

- Most of the businesses in the oldest section of downtown were now *defunct*; the new specialty stores on the other side of the river had put them out of business.

- My already limited interest in cutting the grass was just about *defunct* by the time the grass was actually ready to cut, so I never got around to doing it.

- The long spell of extremely hot weather left my entire garden *defunct*.

Defunct is related to the word function.

DEGENERATE (di JEN uh rayt) *v* to break down; to deteriorate

- The discussion quickly *degenerated* into an argument.

- Over the years, the nice old neighborhood had *degenerated* into a terrible slum.

- The fans' behavior *degenerated* as the game went on.

A person whose behavior has *degenerated* can be referred to as a *degenerate* (di JEN ur it):

- The mood of the party was spoiled when a drunken *degenerate* wandered in from the street.

DEGRADE (di GRAYD) *v* to lower in dignity or status; to corrupt; to deteriorate

- Being made to perform menial duties at the behest of over-bearing male senior partners clearly *degrades* the law firm's female associates.

- The former bank president felt *degraded* working as a teller, but he was unable to find any other job. The former bank president felt that working as a teller was *degrading*.

- The secret potion had *degraded* over the years to the point at which it was no longer capable of turning a person into a frog.

Degradation (deg ruh DAY shun) is the act of *degrading* or the state of being *degraded.*

DEJECTED (di JEK tid) *adj*   depressed; disheartened
- Barney was *dejected* when he heard that Fred had gone to the lodge without him, but he cheered up later when Betty made him some brownies.

- The members of the losing field-hockey team looked *dejected*; their heads were bowed, and they were dragging their sticks.

To be *dejected* is to be in a state of *dejection* (di JEK shun). Rejection often causes *dejection.*

DEPLETE (di PLEET) *v*   to decrease the supply of; to exhaust; to use up
- After three years of careless spending, the young heir had *depleted* his inheritance; he was nearly in danger of having to work for a living. He regretted this *depletion.*

- Irresponsible harvesting has seriously *depleted* the nation's stock of old-growth trees.

- Illness has *depleted* Simone's strength to the point at which she could barely stand without assistance.

Replete means full. The noun is *repletion.*
- Annabelle is a fast typist, but her documents are often *replete* with errors.

DEPLORE (di PLOHR) *v*   to regret; to condemn; to lament
- *Deploring* waste is one thing; actually learning to be less wasteful is another.

- Maria claimed to *deplore* the commercialization of Christmas, but she did spend several thousand dollars on Christmas presents for each of her children.

DERIDE (di RYDE) *v*   to ridicule; to laugh at contemptuously
- Gerald *derided* Diana's driving ability after their hair-raising trip down the twisting mountain road.

- Sportswriters *derided* Columbia's football team, which hadn't won a game in three years.

- The boss *derided* his secretary mercilessly, so she quit her job. She was someone who could not accept *derision* (di RIZH un).

DISPARATE (DIS pur it) *adj*   different; incompatible; unequal
- Our interests were *disparate:* Cathy liked to play with dolls, and I liked to throw her dolls out the window.
- The *disparate* interest groups were united only by their intense dislike of the candidate.
- The novel was difficult to read because the plot consisted of dozens of *disparate* threads that never came together.

The noun form of *disparate* is *disparity* (dih SPAR i tee). *Disparity* means inequality. The opposite of *disparity* is *parity.*

EXONERATE (ig ZAHN uh rayt) *v*   to free completely from blame; to exculpate
- The defendant, who had always claimed he wasn't guilty, expected to be *exonerated* by the testimony of his best friend.
- Our dog was *exonerated* when we discovered that it was in fact the cat that had eaten all the doughnuts.

MAGNANIMOUS (mag NAN uh mus) *adj*   forgiving; not resentful; noble in spirit; generous
- The boxer was *magnanimous* in defeat, telling the sports reporters that his opponent had simply been too talented for him to beat.
- Mrs. Jones *magnanimously* offered the little boy a cookie when he came over to confess that he had accidentally broken her window while playing baseball.

MALAPROPISM (MAL uh prahp iz um) *n*   humorous misuse of a word that sounds similar to the word intended but has a ludicrously different meaning
- In Richard Sheridan's 1775 play, *The Rivals*, a character named Mrs. Malaprop calls someone "the pineapple of politeness" instead of "the pinnacle of politeness." In Mrs. Malaprop's honor, similar verbal boo-boos are known as *malapropisms*. Incidentally, Sheridan derived Mrs. Malaprop's name from *malapropos*, a French import that means "not apropos" or "not appropriate."

- Another master of the *malapropism* was Emily Litella, a character played by Gilda Radner on the television show *Saturday Night Live*, who thought it was ridiculous for people to complain that there was "too much violins" on television.

MALIGNANT (muh LIG nuhnt) *adj*   causing harm
- Many words that start with *mal-* connote evil or harm, just as words that begin with *ben-* generally have good connotations. *Malignant* and *benign* are often used to describe tumors or physical conditions that are either life-threatening or not.

- Lina has had recurring tumors since the operation; we're just glad that none of them have proved *malignant*.

PERIPATETIC (per uh peh TET ik) *adj*   wandering; traveling continually; itinerant
- Groupies are a *peripatetic* bunch, traveling from concert to concert to follow their favorite rock stars.

POSTERITY (pahs TER uh tee) *n*   future generations; descendants; heirs
- Richard necessarily paints for *posterity;* nobody alive has any interest in his pictures.

- There's no point in protecting the world's oil reserves for posterity if we don't also leave *posterity* any air to breathe.

- Samantha is saving her diaries for *posterity;* she hopes that her daughters and granddaughters will enjoy them.

POSTHUMOUS (PAHS chuh mus) *adj*   occurring after one's death; published after the death of the author
- The *posthumous* publication of Ernest Hemingway novels has become a minor literary industry, even though Hemingway clearly had good reasons for keeping the novels unpublished.

REPLETE (ri PLEET) *adj*   completely filled; abounding
- The once-polluted stream was now *replete* with fish of every description.

- The bride wore a magnificent sombrero *replete* with fuzzy dice and campaign buttons.

- Tim ate all nine courses at the wedding banquet. He was filled to the point of *repletion.*

VOCATION (voh KAY shun) *n*   an occupation; a job
- Your *vocation* is what you do for a living.

- If Stan could figure out how to make a *vocation* out of watching television and eating potato chips, he would be one of the most successful people in the world.

- *Vocational* training is job training. Since your *vocation* is your job, your *avocation* is your hobby.

Chapter 8 Practice Exercises

Fill in the Blank
Choose the word that best completes the meaning of the sentence.
Answers can be found on page 227.

1. Jarel was as clever as he was autocratic, and he knew what he could not obtain by legitimate means he could always obtain through _____.
   A) bossiness
   B) contretemps
   C) autonomy
   D) regeneration

2. The visiting professor was so prominent in his _____ that many of our faculty members became nervous in his presence.
   A) antithesis
   B) contraband
   C) vocation
   D) rehabilitation

3. The orator _____ a bizarre economic program whose central tenet was the abolition of all forms of money.
   A) depleted
   B) advocated
   C) apprehended
   D) anthologized

4. Using the word "sciences" for the word "sinuses" is an example of a _____.
   A) dictum
   B) malapropism
   C) malignancy
   D) vocation

5. The actor, pretending to be inebriated, made a _____
   attempt to open his umbrella in a telephone booth.
   A) peripatetic
   B) posthumous
   C) silly
   D) disparate

Synonyms

Match each word on the left with the word most similar in meaning
on the right. Answers can be found on page 228.

1.	opaque	a.	obscure
2.	posterity	b.	guilty
3.	malcontent	c.	exemption
4.	debase	d.	prudent
5.	wise	e.	degrade
6.	enamored	f.	descendants
7.	impugn	g.	captivated
8.	impunity	h.	accuse
9.	culpable	i.	restless
10.	out-of-place	j.	anachronistic

SAT Quick Quiz

Read each passage and answer the questions that follow. Answers can be found on page 228.

The following passage comes from a book of literary criticism by John Gardner.

The language of art critics, and of artists of the kind who pay attention to critics, has become exceedingly odd: not talk about feelings or intellectual affirmations—not talk about moving and
Line surprising twists of plot or wonderful characters and ideas—
5 but sentences full of large words like hermeneutic, heuristic, structuralism, formalism, or opaque language, and full of fine distinctions—for instance those between modernist and post-modernist—that would make even an intelligent cow suspicious. Though more difficult than ever before to read, criticism has
10 become inconsequential.

The trivial has its place, its entertainment value. I can think of no good reason that some people should not specialize in the behavior of the left-side hairs of an elephant's trunk. Even at its best, its most deadly serious, criticism, like art, is partly a
15 game, as all good critics know. My objection is not to the game but to the fact that contemporary critics have for the most part lost track of the point of their game, just as artists, by and large, have lost track of the point of theirs. Fiddling with the hairs on an elephant's nose is indecent when the elephant happens to be
20 standing on the baby.

At least in America, art is not thought capable, these days, of tromping on babies. Yet it does so all the time, and what is worse, it does so with a bland smile. I've watched writers, composers, and painters knocking off their "works" with their
25 left hands. Nice people, most of them. Artists are generally pleasant people, childlike both in love and hate, intending no harm when they turn out bad paintings, compositions or books. Indeed, their ambition guarantees that they will do the best they know how to or think they ought to do. The error is less in their
30 objects than in their objectives. "Art is play, or partly play," they'll tell you with an engaging smile, serving up their non-nutritious

fare with the murderous indifference of a fat cook serving up hamburgers. What they say is true enough, as far as it goes, and nothing is more tiresome than the man who keeps hollering,
35 "Hey, let's be serious!" but that is what we must holler.

In a world where nearly everything that passes for art is tinny and commercial and often, in addition, hollow and academic, I argue—by reason and by banging on the table—for an old-fashioned view of what art is and does and what the
40 fundamental business of critics therefore ought to be. Not that I want joy taken out of the arts; but even frothy entertainment is not harmed by a touch of moral responsibility, at least an evasion of too fashionable simplifications. My basic message is as old as the hills, drawn from Homer, Plato, Aristotle, Dante,
45 and the rest, and standard in Western civilization down through the eighteenth century: one would think all critics and artists should be thoroughly familiar with it, and perhaps many are. But my experience is that in university lecture halls, or in kitchens at midnight, after parties, the traditional view of art strikes most
50 people as strange news.

The traditional view is that true art is moral: it seeks to improve life, not debase it. It seeks to hold off, at least for a while, the twilight of the gods and us. I do not deny that art, like criticism, may legitimately celebrate the trifling. It may joke, or
55 mock, or while away the time. But trivial art has no meaning or value except in the shadows of more serious art, the kind of art that, if you will, makes the world safe for triviality. The art which tends toward destruction, the art of cynics and nihilists, is not properly art at all. Art is essentially serious and beneficial—a
60 game played against chaos and death, against entropy. It is a tragic game, for those who have the wit to take it seriously, because our side must lose: a comic game because only a clown with sawdust brains would take our side and eagerly join in.

Like legitimate art, legitimate criticism is a tragicomic
65 holding action against entropy. Art builds temporary walls against life's leveling force, against the ruin of what is splendidly unnatural in us: consciousness. Art rediscovers, generation by generation, what is necessary to humanness. Criticism restates and clarifies, reinforces the wall.

1

As used in line 6, "opaque" most nearly means

A) dark.

B) obvious.

C) solemn.

D) inscrutable.

2

As used in line 10, "inconsequential" most nearly means

A) irrelevant.

B) vital.

C) careless.

D) suspicious.

3

The author most likely views the "works" of artists (line 24) with

A) magnanimity.

B) apathy.

C) antipathy.

D) indifference.

4

As used in line 30, "objectives" most nearly means

A) artworks.

B) destructions.

C) goals.

D) children.

As used in line 32, "indifference" most nearly means

A) lack of care.

B) concern.

C) hatred.

D) conformity.

As used in line 41, "frothy" most nearly means

A) superficial.

B) foamy.

C) luminous.

D) amorphous.

As used in line 52, "debase" most nearly means

A) degrade.

B) glorify.

C) moralize.

D) deny.

As used in context, "trifling" (line 54) and "trivial" (line 55) most nearly mean

A) magnanimous.

B) exalted.

C) shadowy.

D) unimportant.

As used in line 58, "nihilists" are most likely people who

A) idealize art.

B) seek to destroy the world.

C) seek to undermine traditional modes of artistic expression.

D) are not serious.

As used in line 60, "entropy" most nearly means

A) restoration.

B) disorder.

C) tragedy.

D) frivolity.

As used in line 64, "tragicomic" most nearly means

A) hopeless, and taken up by fools.

B) successful, yet taken up by clowns.

C) serious, yet beneficial.

D) temporary, yet satisfying.

Questions 12–20. *The following series of short passages are similar to those that might appear in a longer SAT Reading passage. Read each one closely and answer the questions that follow.*

But not if she continued to lead such a reckless life. It was becoming her habit to daily court potential disaster by barely sleeping or eating. She had long ago started ignoring the
Line warnings of her family and friends. Her doctor too suggested
5 that the greatest risk to her health at that point was not her diagnosed disease, but the careless lifestyle.

12

As used in line 2, "court" most nearly means

A) legislate.

B) sue.

C) provoke.

D) judge.

If there is one imaginative work of the Romantic era that scientists should pay attention to, it is Mary Shelley's *Frankenstein.* Shelley was familiar with some of the most
Line exciting scientific developments of her day, especially Galvani's
5 experiments with electricity as a life-force. Very much rooted in the science of its day, *Frankenstein* embodies a profound awareness of the larger human context of scientific endeavor.

13

The author's attitude toward Mary Shelley's *Frankenstein* is best described as one of

A) curiosity.

B) indignation.

C) nostalgia.

D) admiration.

Economist Benjamin Grant believes differently. His group, Citizens Against Debt, works to educate people regarding the danger of easy access to loans. As he recently pointed out,

Line "Credit cards have become the new life preserver. How will I pay
5 for that new massage chair? A credit card. How will I pay off my credit card? Another credit card. How will I pay the fine to get released from debtor's prison? Does the court take credit cards?"

14

The tone of Benjamin Grant's comment is best described as

A) laudatory.

B) derisive.

C) dubious.

D) despondent.

Archibald Suttle, quivering, set his teacup on the table and stood up, so he could have free reign to make his next point.

"Well then, there must be thoughts of propriety. Propriety,
Line madam! A woman in this day and age cannot just marry the
5 first stagecoach driver that comes along. A marriage requires, like all things, a firm footing. Not to say love should not enter into the thing, far from it. I am quite fond of my Mrs. Suttle. It was, however, a fondness born of our compatibility in financial matters: we both came from the same place, as it were. Horse
10 before the cart, Elizabeth, not the other way around!"

15

As used in line 3, "propriety" most nearly means

A) appropriateness.

B) self-consciousness.

C) recklessness.

D) fondness.

When director John Guillermin remade *King Kong* in 1976,
he and producer Dino De Laurentis went to great lengths to
convince moviegoers that they were seeing an actual giant
Line ape on the screen in front of them. With a film like 1999's *The*
5 *Matrix*, however, co-directors Andy and Larry Wachowski used
computer generated imagery not intending to produce lifelike
results, but to put a highly stylized accent on the visuals. In one
now-famous fight scene, the female character Trinity is about to
boot a bad guy when she is frozen in mid-air; the camera then
10 sweeps around her, providing a panoramic view of the kick to
come. The Wachowski brothers were not trying to convince
viewers that a person could suspend herself as Trinity does.
Instead, they were trying to come up with a shot that would
make jaws drop.

<hr>

16

The tone of the passage is best characterized as

A) vexed.

B) ambivalent.

C) nihilistic.

D) laudatory.

The witty and ferocious critic—whose frequently negative reviews give the impression he has a vicious appetite for new literature—destroys this demonic portrait when he appears by *Line* appearing before you as a shy and uncomfortable soul. His is of 5 slender limb and deprecating glance. He stammers and makes a painful spectacle of himself when you ask his opinion of the latest best seller or hit play.

17

Which of the following words would most effectively replace "negative" in line 1?

A) powerful.

B) evil.

C) belittling.

D) painful.

18

As used in line 6, "spectacle" most nearly means

A) display.

B) annoyance.

C) triumph.

D) achievement.

19

The passage suggests the critic's reviews are typically

A) disparaging.

B) humorous.

C) diffident.

D) empathetic.

In 1876, Roberts Brothers launched a line of books they called the "No Name Series." At the time, Roberts Brothers was a well-known publisher of such literary luminaries as Robert Louis Stevenson, Walt Whitman, and Louisa May Alcott.

20

As used in line 3, "luminaries" most nearly means

A) tragic heroes.

B) prominent figures.

C) prolific writers.

D) infamous people.

Chapter 8 Answer Key

New Words Drill

1. *Antipodal* means "situated on opposite sides."
2. *Antithesis* is an opposing idea.
3. The root *auto-* means "self," so an *autocrat* wants to manage a country by him- or herself (not in a democratic manner).
4. *Contraband* is negative, as *contra-* means "against." (Contraband is something that is illegally or unethically acquired.)
5. *Contretemps* is negative, as *contra-* means "against." (A contretemps is an argument or dispute; literally, "against time.")
6. To perform a task *autonomously* means to do it by yourself. It is comprised of the roots *auto-* and *nom-*.
7. To *debilitate* is to weaken.
8. To *debunk* is to prove false.
9. If a machine is *defunct,* it is no longer functioning.
10. A *degenerate* person is morally weak or bad. (*De-* is a negative root.)
11. A *dejected* person is sad. (*De-* is a negative root.)
12. *Replete* means "filled up."
13. A *magnanimous* person is generous. The root *magna-* means "great" or "big."
14. A *peripatetic* person would travel a lot. *Peri-* means "around."
15. *Post-* means "after," so *posterity* refers to the people who live after you.
16. *Posthumously* means "after death"; the root *post-* means "after."
17. A *malapropism* is an improper use of a word; *mal-* is negative.
18. A *benign* tumor is the opposite of a *malignant* tumor.
19. *Voc-* pertains to speaking, so your *vocation* is your "calling."
20. An *anthology* is a collection of works, especially written works, so *log-* (words) is more helpful here. *Antho-* is NOT the same as *anthro-*.
21. *Dis-* is negative, so *disparate* groups are dissimilar.
22. *De-* is negative; all of the words (*debase, decry, defame, defile, degrade, deplore,* and *deride*) mean criticizing, harming, or rejecting.

23. *Amo-* means "love"; being *enamored* with something means to be in love with it.
24. *Pugn-* means "fighting" or "attacking," while *pun-* is more similar to "punish." They are both negative roots, but they are not identical. *Impunity* means "immunity from punishment."
25. To *exonerate* means to find innocent. *Ex-* means "outside," so to exonerate literally means that the accused is being taken "outside" of blame.
26. *Exculpate* is similar to the meaning of *exonerate*; both words literally mean to take "outside" of blame.

Fill in the Blank

1. **A** *Autocratic* means behaving like a dictator. Dictators are bossy, so (A) is the best choice. Choice (C) is a good trap, as it contains the same root, but *autonomy* is simply independence.
2. **C** Since he was "prominent" and a "professor," (C) is the best answer. A *vocation* is a job or career.
3. **B** There are not many clues here, so think about which answer choice best describes something that could be done to an economic program. Choice (A) doesn't fit, since that would mean weakening the program. One cannot seize control of a program, so rule out (C). Anthologies are lists or groupings of things, so (D) is also incorrect. An *orator* could certainly "speak" (*voc-*) on behalf of a program, so (B) is the best answer.
4. **B** There is obviously some sort or mistake in the use of these words, so one of the *mal-* answer choices would work well. Choice (C) is far too negative and would imply evil or disease. Choice (B) is the best answer and literally means "not appropriate."
5. **C** To be "inebriated" is to be drunk, so (C) is the best match.

Synonyms

1. a
2. f
3. i
4. e
5. d
6. g
7. h
8. c
9. b
10. j

SAT Quick Quiz

1. **D**   In a vocabulary-in-context question such as this, the obvious definition, (A), is often a trap. Since the words in lines 5 and 6 might be confusing to the average reader, rule out (B). They are not sad, so eliminate (C), which means (D) is the answer. *Inscrutable* means "hard to understand."

2. **A**   In the first paragraph, the author refers to literary criticism as "odd" and difficult to understand, so eliminate (B). Choices (C) and (D) are not supported by the passage. *Inconsequential* literally means "of no consequence," or irrelevant, (A).

3. **C**   In the third paragraph, the author uses disparaging language to describe the artists, so eliminate (A). Since virtually the entire passage is about the author's opinions on this subject, we cannot say he doesn't care, which rules out (B) and (D). This leaves you with (C), which means hatred or distaste.

4. **C**   Choice (A) is definitely a trap. Just because these are artists, that does not mean that "objectives" are artworks. Choice (B) sounds much too negative, and (D) is unsupported by the passage. The answer is (C).

5. **A**   It's a funny comparison, but a "fat cook" serving "non-nutritious fare" would suggest a "lack of care." In other words, the fat cook does not care about the quality of the food, since he himself is well fed. Choice (A) is correct.

6. **A** Always be suspicious of the most obvious definitions. Choice (B) is definitely a trap. Choices (C) and (D) are not supported by the passage. *Frothy* entertainment would be shallow, so (A) is a good match and the correct answer.

7. **A** Lines 51–52 state that the traditional view of art holds that it "seeks to improve life, not debase it." So, *debasing* must be the opposite of "improving." Choices (A) and (D) are close, but *denying* is simply a rejection of a fact, not a weakening of something.

8. **D** The clue "no meaning or value" (lines 55–56) makes (D) the clear choice here.

9. **C** According to the passage, the art of nihilists "tends toward destruction," but (B) is far too literal. Since the passage contrasts traditional views of art with more modern views, (C) is the correct answer.

10. **B** Look at the sentence and surrounding sentences for clues. "Chaos and death" (line 60) should point you to the answer, which is (B), *entropy.*

11. **A** Look to the end of the previous paragraph, which states that "our side must lose…because only a clown with sawdust brains would take our side and eagerly join in" (lines 62–63). The answer is (A).

12. **C** As with prior examples, obvious definitions of simple-looking words are almost always trap answers. Choices (A), (B), and (D) are all words associated with a courtroom, but they are incorrect. The answer is (C), *provoke.*

13. **D** The author uses words like "imaginative" and "profound" to describe *Frankenstein*, which reflects *admiration,* (D).

14. **B** If a person is continuously relying on credit cards to the point of going to debtor's prison, Grant would view this as a ridiculous situation. *Derisive*, (B), means expressing ridicule, so it is the best match.

15. **A** Suttle believes that "A woman in this day and age cannot just marry the first stagecoach driver that comes along" and that "A marriage requires, like all things, a firm footing." Therefore, Suttle cares about the rightness or *appropriateness* of one's actions, which matches (A).

16. **D** There is no indication in the passage that the author dislikes the movie. If anything, the descriptions sound fun and exciting. Therefore, the best match is (D), *laudatory,* which means to express praise.

17. **C**   The critic is described in the first sentence as "ferocious" and "vicious," which is in line with (C), *belittling.*

18. **A**   The critic "stammers" (line 6) and is "shy" (line 4), so rule out (C) and (D). Choice (B) is close, but not supported by the passage. The correct answer is (A), *display.*

19. **A**   Look back to the explanation for question 17. The answer to that question was *belittling,* which is closest in meaning to *disparaging,* (A).

20. **B**   Pat yourself on the back if you recognized the root *lum-.* A luminary is a prominent person, so (B) is correct. (*Infamous* refers to being famous for something bad.)

Chapter 8 Bonus Word List

DEPRECATE (DEP ruh kayt) *v*   to express disapproval of
- To *deprecate* a colleague's work is to risk making yourself unwelcome in your colleague's office.
- "This stinks!" is a *deprecating* remark.
- The critic's *deprecating* comments about my new novel put me in a bad mood for an entire month.
- To be *self-deprecating* is to belittle one's own efforts, sometimes in the hope that someone else will say, "No, you're wonderful!"

NIHILISM (NYE uh liz um) *n*   the belief that there are no values or morals in the universe
- A *nihilist* does not believe in any objective standards of right or wrong.

OPAQUE (oh PAYK) *adj*   impossible to see through; impossible to understand
- The windows in the movie star's house were made not of glass but of some *opaque* material intended to keep his fans from spying on him.
- We tried to figure out what Horace was thinking, but his expression was *opaque:* It revealed nothing.
- Jerry's mind, assuming he had one, was *opaque.*
- The statement was *opaque;* no one could make anything of it.

The noun form of *opaque* is *opacity* (oh PAS uh tee).

PROPRIETY (pruh PRYE uh tee) *n*   properness; good manners
- The old lady viewed the little girl's failure to curtsy as a flagrant breach of *propriety.* She did not approve of or countenance such *improprieties.*
- *Propriety* prevented the young man from trashing the town in celebration of his unexpected acceptance by the college of his choice.

Propriety derives from *proper,* not *property,* and should not be confused with *proprietary.*

CHAPTER 9

Cumulative Drills

Time for Review!

Now it's time to see how you have progressed since Chapter 1 and how well you have understood the material in this book. Complete the exercises in this chapter and then check your answers against the answer key, which starts on page 259.

Word Relationships

Decide whether each pair of words below is roughly similar (S) in meaning, roughly opposite (O) in meaning, or unrelated (U) to each other. Answers can be found on page 259.

Set 1

1. posthumously	replete	_____
2. legacy	posterity	_____
3. aptitude	ineptitude	_____
4. vocation	provocation	_____
5. ascertain	determine	_____
6. assimilate	isolate	_____
7. astute	smart	_____
8. polarized	antipodal	_____
9. asylum	danger	_____
10. callous	benevolent	_____

Set 2

1. pragmatic	automatic	_____
2. penitent	penchant	_____
3. proliferate	grow	_____
4. amenable	atheist	_____
5. prolific	productive	_____
6. reticent	reserved	_____
7. peripatetic	traveling	_____
8. rudimentary	sophisticated	_____
9. inferior	subservient	_____
10. flaunt	sagacious	_____

Set 3

1. invoke	evoke	_____
2. extrovert	introvert	_____
3. bluster	shyness	_____
4. castigate	deplore	_____
5. debilitate	rehabilitate	_____
6. placid	frantic	_____
7. debase	defile	_____
8. magnificent	grand	_____
9. grandiloquent	bombastic	_____
10. malefactor	benefactor	_____

Set 4

1. expedite	accelerate	_____
2. fiscal	cosmopolitan	_____
3. flagrant	abstruse	_____
4. fledgling	immature	_____
5. laudatory	substandard	_____
6. pedantic	strict	_____
7. reciprocation	renovation	_____
8. flaunt	show	_____
9. antithesis	epitome	_____
10. lavish	modest	_____

Odd Man Out

Each row below consists of four words, three of which are related in meaning. Circle or underline the word that does not fit. Answers can be found on page 260.

Set 1

1. uniform · erudite · knowledgeable · wise
2. flaunt · malign · hate · criticize
3. gaffe · blunder · mistake · indolence
4. weak · tenuous · insolent · flimsy
5. insular · insulated · isolated · insured
6. disparate · different · distinct · omnipresent
7. apprehensive · despondent · nervous · fearful
8. cerebral · strong · omnipotent · robust
9. malinger · linger · avoid · pretend
10. pedantic · scholarly · preachy · volitional

Set 2

1. contiguous · continuous · bordering · corrugated
2. reprove · scrutinize · censure · rebuke
3. degrade · delineate · denounce · deride
4. defame · depreciate · disparage · despair
5. bendable · strong · tenuous · weak
6. free · exonerate · qualify · exculpate
7. worldly · cosmopolitan · wealthy · sophisticated
8. epitome · example · model · greatness
9. exhausting · exorbitant · excessive · expensive
10. circumlocution · fallacy · equivocation · penchant

Fill in the Blank

Choose the word that best completes the meaning of each sentence. Answers can be found on page 260.

1. The Sandersons viewed the flaming image of the witch, which hovered above their house for thirteen days, as a _____ sign of evil.
   A) malignant
   B) specious
   C) peripheral
   D) tentative

2. There was nothing _____ about Herbert's scientific theories; in fact, they were quite shallow.
   A) superficial
   B) vociferous
   C) tenuous
   D) erudite

3. The _____ author turned out a new book every week of her adult life.
   A) prolific
   B) explicit
   C) abstruse
   D) implicit

4. The _____ girls stubbornly refused to call off their rock fight, despite the pleadings of their mothers.
   A) intractable
   B) placable
   C) autocratic
   D) bombastic

5. Hal's disappointed wife _____ him for being a lazy, foul-smelling, obnoxious slob.
   A) expatriated
   B) decried
   C) flaunted
   D) deduced

SAT Quick Quiz

Read the passages and answer the questions that follow. Answers can be found on page 261.

The following passage discusses the annexation of Hawaii in the late nineteenth century.

On January 28, 1893, Americans read in their evening newspapers a bulletin from Honolulu, Hawaii. Two weeks earlier, said the news report, a group of American residents had
Line overthrown a young native queen and formed a provisional
5 government. Marines from the *U.S.S. Boston* had landed at the request of the American minister in order to protect lives and property. Violence had ended quickly. The rebels were in full control and were said to have enthusiastic support from the populace. Most noteworthy of all, they had announced the
10 intention of asking the United States to annex the islands.

The proposal was not as startling as it might have seemed. Most of the large landowners in the islands were Americans or the children of Americans. So too were the men who grew, refined, and shipped the sugar that was Hawaii's principal
15 export. In addition, many of the kingdom's Protestant clergymen, lawyers, bankers, factory owners, and other leading personages were also American citizens. Though numbering only two thousand of the island's total population of around ninety thousand, these Americans had already given Hawaii the
20 appearance of a colony. This influence could be seen as far back as 1854 when they nearly persuaded a native monarch to request annexation by the United States. Subsequently, the American element helped secure tariff reciprocity from the United States while the island ceded a naval station to the United States. Such
25 measures sparked enough concern by the United States to lead Presidents from Tyler on down to periodically warn European powers against meddling in Hawaiian affairs. Thus, by 1893, the new proposal might have been characterized as simply a plan to annex a state already Americanized and virtually a protectorate.
30 Nonetheless, the proposition came unexpectedly, and neither politicians nor journalists knew quite what to make

of it. Editorials and comments from Capitol Hill were at first noncommittal. The molders of public opinion seemed intent on learning what mold the public wanted.

35   San Francisco's leading Republican and Democratic dailies, the *Chronicle* and *Examiner*, declared that Hawaii should certainly be accepted as a state. On January 29, the *Chronicle* reported a poll of local businessmen demonstrating overwhelming support for this view. Some businessmen focused
40 on potential profits. Claus Spreckels, for example, who owned Hawaii's largest sugar plantation, hoped to obtain the two-cent-a-pound bounty paid by the United States government to domestic sugar producers. In addition, he anticipated increased freight for his Oceanic Steamship line as more plentiful and
45 cheaper raw sugar for his California Sugar Refinery Company.

1

As used in line 4, "provisional" most nearly means

A) official.

B) permanent.

C) temporary.

D) cruel.

2

As used in line 10, "annex" most nearly means

A) abandon.

B) attach.

C) abuse.

D) liberate.

As used in line 24, "ceded" most nearly means

A) gave up.

B) captured.

C) planted.

D) attacked.

As used in line 27, "meddling" most nearly means

A) helping.

B) dictating.

C) attaching.

D) interfering.

As used in line 29, "protectorate" most nearly means

A) a free country.

B) a country protected from natural disasters.

C) a country subject to partial control by another country.

D) a country subject to cruel treatment by invaders.

As used in line 30, "proposition" most nearly means

A) indecent offer.

B) proposal.

C) rejected offer.

D) doomed plan.

7

As used in line 33, "noncommittal" most nearly means

A) dubious.

B) antipathetic.

C) malevolent.

D) pugnacious.

8

A newspaper might be named the *Chronicle* (line 38) because it

A) often expresses biased points of view.

B) is popular among readers.

C) keeps track of local events.

D) is primarily concerned with making a profit.

9

As used in line 42, "bounty" most nearly means

A) reward.

B) punishment.

C) inducement.

D) plentiful amount.

Questions 10–17. *The following series of short passages are similar to those that might appear in a longer SAT Reading passage. Read each one closely and answer the questions that follow.*

Our understanding of the composition of matter has changed radically in the past one hundred years. Before Ernest Rutherford posited the existence of protons, neutrons, and electrons in 1911, even the most accomplished scientist conceived of the atom as the smallest possible unit of matter. There was nothing smaller. Now, we know that there are myriad subatomic particles, ranging from protons and electrons to quarks and neutrinos.

10

As used in line 6, "myriad" most nearly means

A) small number of.

B) large number of.

C) insignificant number of.

D) confusing array of.

It has been documented that the best chess players do not view the playing pieces in isolation, noting their locations individually. Rather, they visualize sections of the chessboard in a process known as chunking; they may not remember exactly where each piece is on the board, but they know the position of each piece relative to the others. Researchers in artificial intelligence have tried to duplicate this sort of vision in their chess-playing computer programs, with varying degrees of success. In an attempt to beat the human players at their own game, the programmers have turned away from the computer's traditional strength—the ability to perform an astonishing number of calculations quickly and flawlessly—and begun to model their programs after the cerebral structures of the most successful humans.

Line appears beside line 4, *5* beside line 5, *10* beside line 10.

11

As used in line 13, "cerebral" most nearly means

A) calibrated.

B) spiritual.

C) cutthroat.

D) mental.

The following passage is adapted from a novel set in the early twentieth century. Lily Bart, a New York socialite, is speaking with her friend Lawrence Selden about some of the differences between the lives led by women and men.

Lily sank with a sigh into one of the shabby leather chairs.

"How delicious to have a place like this all to one's self! What a miserable thing it is to be a woman." She leaned back in a
Line luxury of discontent.

5 Selden was rummaging in a cupboard for the cake.

"Even women," he said, "have been known to enjoy the privileges of a flat."

"Oh, governesses—or widows. But not girls—not poor, miserable, marriageable girls!"

12

Lily's tone is one of

A) antipathy.

B) apathy.

C) deference.

D) self-pity.

I grew up believing that I hated tomatoes. I used to describe the raw fruit as tasting like curdled water and preferred tomato sauce from a can. But it was not by accident that the tomato
Line rapidly insinuated itself into the world's cuisines after 1492: it
5 grows like a weed, and wherever this weed took root, locals fell in love with it.

13

As used in line 4, "insinuated" most nearly means

A) inserted.

B) interfered.

C) removed.

D) killed.

The haiku's relative simplicity explains its popular use worldwide as a means to introduce young children to poetry. The brief Japanese poem consists of three lines with a set
Line number of syllables for each line. But the form is not as simple
5 as it seems. The poem must also describe a single event taking place in the present, as well as make reference to the four seasons. Although a haiku can seem timeless, its reference to the changes in nature serves to indirectly highlight the ephemeral quality of life.

14

As used in line 8, "ephemeral" most nearly means

A) eternal.

B) endless.

C) short-lived.

D) frivolous.

A recent theory, which is still contested, claims that disease can travel from one continent to another in dust clouds. According to the theory, the Sahara Desert, which has grown
Line over the past thirty years due to the near constant drought
5 conditions in northern Africa, is polluted with pesticides and laced with diseases from human and animal waste. The dust from the desert, when picked up by wind, can travel thousands of miles, carrying the disease-laden particles around the world.

15

If the theory mentioned in line 1 is controversial, then "contested" most nearly means

A) competed.

B) debated.

C) deplored.

D) debased.

The nuns of Mankato raise interesting questions about how the brain functions as we age. These women, many of whom are older than ninety, believe that they must avoid an idle mind, and so they challenge themselves doggedly. Common leisure activities among the nuns include vocabulary quizzes, puzzles, and debates. They hold seminars on current events, keep journals, and teach, many well into their eighties and nineties. They also suffer far fewer cases of dementia, Alzheimer's, and other brain diseases than does the general public.

Line

5

16

The passage suggests that the nuns of Mankato are very

A) amiable.

B) indolent.

C) benevolent.

D) erudite.

People in the Bay Area were talkative, I think, because they weren't afraid of being boring. In Ireland, things are rather different. Being boring is an unforgivable conversational sin. The fear of saying something dull makes some people seize up like clams and everyone else speak in nervous banter. In conversation, it's also forbidden to be serious. No one will listen to what you say if you say it with a straight face: you have to tack a smirk or a joke or a put-down onto everything. There is a tremendous pressure to be funny at all times, especially during introductions.

Line

5

17

Which word would be a valid substitute for "talkative" in line 1?

A) Callous

B) Evocative

C) Provocative

D) Loquacious

The following passage is adapted from Mark Twain's memoir, *Life on the Mississippi* (1883). Twain worked for several years as a steamboat pilot on the Mississippi River before becoming a writer.

Now when I had mastered the language of this water and had come to know every trifling feature that bordered the great river as familiarly as I knew the letters of the alphabet, I had made a
Line valuable acquisition. But I had lost something, too. I had lost
5 something which could never be restored to me while I lived. All the grace, the beauty, the poetry had gone out of the majestic river! I still keep in mind a certain wonderful sunset which I witnessed when steamboating was new to me. A broad expanse of the river was turned to blood; in the middle distance the red
10 hue brightened into gold, through which a solitary log came floating, black and conspicuous; in one place a long, slanting mark lay sparkling upon the water; in another the surface was broken by boiling, tumbling rings, that were as many-tinted as an opal; where the ruddy flush was faintest, was a smooth spot
15 that was covered with graceful circles and radiating lines, ever so delicately traced; the shore on our left was densely wooded, and the somber shadow that fell from this forest was broken in one place by a long, ruffled trail that shone like silver; and high above the forest wall a clean-stemmed dead tree waved a single leafy
20 bough that glowed like a flame in the unobstructed splendor that was flowing from the sun. There were graceful curves, reflected images, woody heights, soft distances; and over the whole scene, far and near, the dissolving lights drifted steadily, enriching it, every passing moment, with new marvels of coloring.
25 I stood like one bewitched. I drank it in, in a speechless rapture. The world was new to me, and I had never seen anything like this at home. But as I have said, a day came when I began to cease from noting the glories and the charms which the moon and the sun and the twilight wrought upon the river's
30 face; another day came when I ceased altogether to note them. Then, if that sunset scene had been repeated, I should have looked upon it without rapture, and should have commented upon it, inwardly, in this fashion: This sun means that we are going to have wind tomorrow; that floating log means that the

river is rising, small thanks to it; that slanting mark on the water refers to a bluff reef which is going to kill somebody's steamboat one of these nights, if it keeps on stretching out like that; those tumbling "boils" show a dissolving bar and a changing channel there; the lines and circles in the slick water over yonder are a
40 warning that that troublesome place is shoaling up dangerously; that silver streak in the shadow of the forest is the "break" from a new snag, and he has located himself in the very best place he could have found to fish for steamboats; that tall dead tree, with a single living branch, is not going to last long, and then how is a
45 body ever going to get through this blind place at night without the friendly old landmark?

No, the romance and the beauty were all gone from the river. All the value any feature of it had for me now was the amount of usefulness it could furnish toward compassing the safe piloting
50 of a steamboat. Since those days, I have pitied doctors from my heart. What does the lovely flush in a beauty's cheek mean to a doctor but a "break" that ripples above some deadly disease? Are not all her visible charms sown thick with what are to him the signs and symbols of hidden decay? Does he ever see her beauty
55 at all, or doesn't he simply view her professionally, and comment upon her unwholesome condition all to himself? And doesn't he sometimes wonder whether he has gained most or lost most by learning his trade?

18

As used in line 4, "acquisition" most nearly means

A) conquest.

B) beauty.

C) gain.

D) question.

The author's attitude toward the "sunset scene" (line 31) after working on the river for several years is best described as

A) reticent.

B) nostalgic.

C) sophomoric.

D) pragmatic.

As used in line 11, "conspicuous" most nearly means

A) hidden.

B) noticeable.

C) ugly.

D) destroyed.

As used in line 17, "somber" most nearly means

A) despondent.

B) cheerful.

C) consistent.

D) vital.

As used in line 20, "splendor" most nearly means

A) destruction.

B) melancholy.

C) boredom.

D) beauty.

As used in line 25, "bewitched" most nearly means

A) cursed.

B) fascinated.

C) bored.

D) fictionalized.

As used in line 29, "wrought" most nearly means

A) fought.

B) bought.

C) taught.

D) made.

Which of the following words could be substituted for "yonder" (line 39) without changing the meaning of the sentence?

A) This

B) That

C) There

D) Who

The primary purpose of the passage is to show that technical knowledge can detract from *aesthetic* appreciation. Based on the context of the passage, "aesthetic" most nearly means

A) artful.

B) pertaining to beauty or art.

C) majestic.

D) appreciation of nature.

Defining a uniquely American educational system was one of the challenges faced by the Revolutionary generation. The following passage discusses the views on education of two of America's most important 18th-century political figures.

Benjamin Franklin and Thomas Jefferson shared basic ideas about the importance of education and its social implications in the early American Republic because both were greatly
Line influenced by the liberal Enlightenment thinkers, but they
5 differed on more specific points of organization, funding, and subject matter.

Benjamin Franklin's outlook on education was tempered by his humble background and his rise to fame through self-motivation and hard work. He did not feel that publicly funded
10 education was necessary because personal ability and initiative to educate oneself would be (as it had been in his case) enough to drive the most worthy candidates to the top. Education beyond the elementary level, he claimed, was simply not necessary or desirable to all people. Franklin was critical of a
15 strictly classical education, for he felt it served no purpose in the new era and perpetuated the elitist trend in higher education, a trend which ran counter to the democratic ideals of the age. His model for a new private academy, as put forth in his "Proposals Relating to the Education of Youth in Pennsylvania" of 1743,
20 answered growing middle class needs while still including traditional elements of the classical model. The curriculum of the private academy would reflect the current trends of the day—empiricism, sense realism, and science—as well as Franklin's personal utilitarian and commercial interests.
25 True to his deistic inclinations, scientific study was included in the curriculum, as were basic moral principles, but sectarian religious views were not.

In contrast to Franklin, whose ideas against publicly funded education found a wide audience, Thomas Jefferson
30 felt that universal education was imperative for democratic participation in community development; therefore, he strongly advocated state control of secular education. Like Franklin, Jefferson acknowledged that there were those who had a greater predilection for scholarship, but while Franklin seemed content

to let the more able students scramble to the top on their own with no state assistance, Jefferson wanted the state to fund secondary schooling for more academically capable youth, as well as universal elementary education for all children. Jefferson also strongly advocated the retention of the classical curriculum in higher education. In 1779 he tried unsuccessfully to reform the college of William and Mary, which at that time offered only religious instruction for future church leaders and a liberal curriculum for the aristocracy. Jefferson felt that a classical education was still the most appropriate for the training of leaders who must understand basics of democracy and human political interaction; in short, he wanted education for civic leadership to be part of university curriculum. Jefferson, like the French philosophers Condorcet and Rousseau before him, was a little ahead of his time on this issue; eventually his models for both state-supported, secular education and university curricula for civic leadership were more widely accepted in the nineteenth century than they were in his own time.

Overall, the disparities between the educational views of Jefferson and Franklin are attributable in large part to the fact that the two men concerned themselves with different elements of education, even though they were influenced by the same philosophical beliefs. Franklin's efforts targeted secondary schooling, while Jefferson concerned himself with improving higher level curriculum. Franklin's reforms benefited the commercial classes, with whom he had many contacts and a personal interest in assisting, while the efforts of Jefferson, who mistrusted capitalism and the mercantile mentality, were intended to improve the lot of the democratic political elite.

However, there is still much the two men had in common; both Franklin and Jefferson envisioned the building of a democratic society in the new Republic. They were both against strong central government, religious authoritarianism, and elitism in public institutions. They both felt that the educational structure should serve the greater needs of society and produce citizens, not just religious leaders and aristocrats. Both were also hostile to organized religion because European history had already shown the kind of violence and cultural

stagnation that resulted from the dogmatic, intolerant strains of religious sectarianism. A democratic state by definition
75 required a citizenry that identified itself as members of a larger community—of humanity—as opposed to a specific religious group. This was one of the primary goals of Enlightenment education in America—to educate all people in order to enable them to fulfill their civic responsibilities.

27

As used in line 2, "implications" most nearly means

A) hints.

B) ramifications.

C) intellectualizations.

D) dangers.

28

As used in line 7, "tempered" most nearly means

A) formed.

B) angered.

C) timed.

D) hindered.

29

As used in line 16, "elitist" most nearly means

A) wealthy person.

B) uneducated person.

C) privileged person.

D) traditional person.

As used in line 23, "empiricism" most nearly means

A) faith.

B) religious zeal.

C) scientific observation.

D) diligence.

As used in line 24, "utilitarian" most nearly means

A) practical.

B) impractical.

C) profitable.

D) unprofitable.

As used in line 25, "deistic" most nearly means

A) rejecting morality.

B) elevating science above all other concerns.

C) promoting sectarian religious views.

D) allowing for variations in religious belief.

As used in line 30, "imperative" most nearly means

A) necessary.

B) unnecessary.

C) optional.

D) detrimental to.

As used in line 32, "secular" most nearly means

A) religious.

B) nonreligious.

C) scientific.

D) artistic.

As used in line 34, "predilection" most nearly means

A) aptitude.

B) ineptitude.

C) foreknowledge.

D) speed.

As used in line 39, "advocated" most nearly means

A) spoke out against.

B) called out.

C) summoned.

D) spoke in favor of.

As used in line 53, "disparities" most nearly means

A) similarities.

B) differences.

C) sad events.

D) conflicts.

Which of the following phrases most relates to capitalism (line 62)?

A) "the same philosophical beliefs" (lines 56-57)

B) "secondary schooling" (lines 57-58)

C) "the commercial classes" (lines 59-60)

D) "political elite" (line 63)

As used in line 73, "stagnation" most nearly means

A) flowering.

B) lack of growth.

C) embrace of knowledge.

D) civic responsibility.

As used in line 73, "dogmatic" most nearly means

A) open-minded.

B) stubborn.

C) curious.

D) violent.

Chapter 9 Answer Key

Word Relationships

Set 1

1. U
2. S
3. O
4. U
5. S
6. O
7. S
8. S
9. O
10. O

Set 2

1. U
2. U
3. S
4. U
5. S
6. S
7. S
8. O
9. S
10. U

Set 3

1. S
2. O
3. O
4. S
5. O
6. O
7. S
8. S
9. S
10. O

Set 4

1. S
2. U
3. U
4. S
5. O
6. S
7. U
8. S
9. O
10. O

Odd Man Out

Set 1

1. uniform
2. flaunt
3. indolence
4. insolent
5. insured
6. omnipresent
7. despondent
8. cerebral
9. linger
10. volitional

Set 2

1. corrugated
2. scrutinize
3. delineate
4. despair
5. strong
6. qualify
7. wealthy
8. greatness
9. exhausting
10. penchant

Fill in the Blank

1. **A** The clue "evil" means that you need to look for a negative word. *Mal-* is the right root for this meaning, so (A) is the answer.

2. **D** You need a word that means the opposite of "shallow," so rule out (A). Choice (D) means knowledgeable or intellectual, which is the best match and the correct answer.

3. **A** Writing a new book every week would mean producing lots of material in a short time. A word describing this is (A), *prolific,* which refers to being plentiful or present in large quantities.

4. **A** The clue here is "stubbornly." *Intractable* means "stubborn," so (A) is the correct answer.

5. **B** Hal's wife is "disappointed." The answer is (B), *decried,* which means "criticized" or "denounced." (Be careful in this question; don't just look for negative words. *De-* words are almost always negative, but (D) is an exception.)

SAT Quick Quiz

1. **C** The events in the first paragraph happen suddenly and quickly, so it makes sense that the government was only *temporary,* (C). Later the passage states that the purpose of the uprising was to annex Hawaii (the more permanent solution).

2. **B** The topic of the passage is Hawaii becoming a state, *attaching* it to the rest of the United States. This is the process of annexation. Choice (B) is the answer.

3. **A** Since the island is ceding a naval station to the United States (line 24), only (A) fits.

4. **D** The passage states that presidents "warn...against" meddling, so the word must mean something negative. Choice (A) is positive and (C) is neutral, so eliminate them. In context, the choice that works is (D), *interfering.*

5. **C** Hawaii has been "Americanized," which means it has been subject to the influence of the United States. In this context, (A) does not exactly work, and (B) does not make sense. Between (C) and (D), (C) is the better answer because (D) is much too extreme.

6. **B** The previous paragraph describes a "new proposal" and "a plan to annex" Hawaii, which matches (B). Choices (C) and (D) are not supported by the text, and there is nothing in the passage that indicates the proposal is "indecent," which eliminates (A).

7. **A** Look at the sentence that follows *noncommittal:* "The molders of public opinion seemed intent on learning what mold the public wanted." This suggests they did not have a strong opinion of their own. The best answer here is therefore (A), *dubious,* which means "doubtful."

8. **C** *Chron-* means "time," so a *chronicle* would keep track of events happening in time. The correct answer is (C).

9. **A** The *bounty* is something "paid by the United States government to domestic sugar producers," and Spreckels expects "profits" (line 40). Choice (C) is close, but *inducement* implies force. Choice (D) is a trap, since it is an alternative definition of *bounty.* The correct answer is (A).

10. **B** The particles range "from protons and electrons to quarks and neutrinos," which suggests that there are a large number of them. The answer is (B).

11. **D**   Chess is a mental game, and the purpose of the computers is to provide artificial "intelligence." These clues should help you select (D), *mental,* as the answer.

12. **D**   Lily sinks "with a sigh" into one of the shabby leather chairs. She then says, "What a miserable thing it is to be a woman" and "leaned back in a luxury of discontent." This suggests a tone of *self-pity,* which is (D).

13. **A**   The tomato was introduced into world cuisines after 1492. Choices (B), (C), and (D) are far too negative. The answer is (A).

14. **C**   The beginning of the last sentence states, "Although a haiku can seem timeless...." The word *although* signals a shift in direction. Therefore, *ephemeral* must mean the opposite of *timeless.* Choice (C), *short-lived,* is the correct answer.

15. **B**   This time, the clue is within the question itself. A *controversial* theory is one that would be *debated,* (B). Choices (C) and (D) are far too negative and not supported by the passage, and (A) does not make sense in context.

16. **D**   Use Process of Elimination. There is no evidence that the nuns are *friendly,* (A), or *benevolent,* (C). They are definitely not *lazy,* (B), since they are engaged in so many activities. Choice (D), *erudite,* is the most reasonable answer, as many of their activities are intellectual in nature.

17. **D**   Remember your roots! *Loq-* refers to speaking, and *loquacious* means "talking a lot." *Voc-* in (B) and (C) refers to speaking as well, but not to an excessive degree. Choice (D) is correct.

18. **C**   In lines 3 and 4, the author states that he "had made a valuable acquisition...[but] had lost something, too." So, an acquisition must be the opposite of a loss, which is (C), *gain.*

19. **D**   The author states that he looked upon the sunset scene "without rapture [happiness]" and goes on to talk about merely factual details about the river. A *pragmatic* person thinks only of practical details around an issue and tends not to romanticize. Therefore, (D) is the answer.

20. **B**   *Conspicuous* refers to "solitary log" that the author sees clearly. Therefore, (B) is the most logical answer.

21. **A** We don't usually think of shadows as having cheerful characteristics, so eliminate (A). Shadows are often associated with a mood that is dark and potentially depressing. Choice (A), *despondent,* is the closest match, as it means "sad."

22. **D** This section of the passage has an abundance of very positive language: "glowed like a flame"; "graceful curves"; "marvels of coloring"; "I stood like one bewitched. I drank it in, in a speechless rapture." Choices (A), (B), and (C) are all negative words. The answer is (D).

23. **B** Look back to the explanation for question 22. This part of the passage is filled with positive language extolling nature. The answer here is (B), *fascinated.*

24. **D** Put the sentence in your own words: The moon and the sun would "make" the river look a certain way. Therefore, the answer is (D).

25. **C** Substitute each answer choice into the sentence. The only one that works is (C).

26. **B** Half of the passage is about the author's poetic appreciation of the river's beauty, while the other half shows that the author eventually became indifferent to its beauty. Choice (B) is closest to this meaning. Choice (D) is a good trap, but the author's sentiments do not only apply to nature (check the last paragraph). Choice (A) might sound tempting, but the question is not asking about the nature of the author's appreciation; it is asking about what the author appreciated.

27. **B** Choice (A) is a good trap if you are simply looking at the word, but always check the context. In the context of the passage, the word means *ramifications,* (B).

28. **A** Franklin's outlook was *formed* by his upbringing. The answer is (A).

29. **C** A strictly classical education would have no practical purpose, making it most appealing to the already well-educated or highly intelligent. Therefore, (C), *privileged,* is correct. Choice (A) is tempting, but wealth is not directly connected to one's level of education.

30. **C** In line 23, "empiricism" is matched up with "sense realism and science." This is closest in meaning to *scientific observation,* (C).

31. **A** In line 24, "utilitarian" is paired up with "commercial," so Franklin is interested in a type of education that has *practical* applications. This matches (A).

32. **D** According to this paragraph, "sectarian religious views were not" included in the curriculum. "Sectarian" religious views would be those limited only to a particular point of view. In contrast, a *deistic* view is one that allows for variations, (D).

33. **A** Jefferson "strongly advocated state control of secular education," which suggests he felt it was necessary. Therefore, (A) is the correct answer.

34. **B** Reread the sentence, paying attention to the clue ("state control"), and then use Process of Elimination. What would state-controlled education probably be most like? Choices (A), (C), and (D) don't answer that question, so eliminate them. Choice (B), *nonreligious,* is correct.

35. **A** Again, pay attention to context. Students with a "greater predilection for scholarship" are related to the "more able students" referenced in line 35 and the "more academically capable youth" in line 37. The word closest to *able* and *capable* is (A), *aptitude,* which is the correct answer.

36. **D** Remember your roots from Chapter 2! *Voc-* refers to speaking, so narrow the choices down to (A) and (D). Based on the context of the passage, you should understand that Jefferson was in favor of classical education. Therefore, the answer is (D).

37. **B** *Dis-* is a negative root, so eliminate (A). In context, (C) does not make sense, so eliminate it. You're left with (B) and (D). Based on the context of the passage, (D) is too strong; the correct answer is (B).

38. **C** Read the sentence in which *capitalism* appears to get a feel for the context. The first half of the sentence refers to the "commercial classes" favored by Franklin's reforms; the second half of the sentence begins with the word *while,* which signals a transition. The second part of the sentence also says that Jefferson "mistrusted capitalism" and instead favored the "political elite," which puts capitalism and the political elite in contrast to each other. From this context, you can infer that capitalism and the "commercial classes" are related. The answer is (C).

39. **B** Go back to the sentence in which the word appears. Notice the negative words like "violence," "dogmatic," and "intolerant." You can therefore infer that *stagnation* is also a negative word. Now go back to the answer choices. *Flowering, embrace of knowledge,* and *civic responsibility* are all positive words and phrases. Therefore, the only choice that makes sense is (B), *lack of growth.*

40. **B** Use the previous question and explanation to help you with this one. You can eliminate (A) and (C), which are too positive for the context. You're left with *stubborn* and *violent.* Which word best describes "religious sectarianism" (line 74)? *Violent* is too extreme here, so the answer is (B), *stubborn.* (*Dogmatic* can be used to describe someone who is unwavering in a belief.)

Chapter 9 Word List

ACQUISITIVE (uh KWIZ uh tiv) *adj* seeking or tending to acquire; greedy

- Children are naturally *acquisitive;* when they see something, they want it, and when they want something, they take it.

- The auctioneer tried to make the grandfather clock sound interesting and valuable, but no one in the room was in an *acquisitive* mood, and the clock went unsold.

- Johnny's natural *acquisitiveness* made it impossible for him to leave the junkyard empty-handed.

ANNEX (uh NEKS) *v* to add or attach
- Old McDonald increased the size of his farm by *annexing* an adjoining field.

A small connecting structure added to a building is often called an *annex* (AN eks).
- The *annex* of the elementary school had a small gymnasium.

CAPITALISM (KAP uh tuh liz um) *n* an economic system in which businesses are owned by private citizens (not by the government) and in which the resulting products and services are sold with relatively little government control
- The American economy is *capitalist*. If you want to start a company to sell signed photographs of yourself, you can. You, not the government, would decide how much you would charge for the pictures. Your success or failure would depend on how many people decided to buy your pictures.

DOGMATIC (dawg MAT ik) *adj* arrogantly assertive of unproven ideas; stubbornly claiming that something (often a system of beliefs) is beyond dispute

A *dogma* is a belief. A *dogmatic* person, however, is stubbornly convinced of his beliefs.
- Marty is *dogmatic* on the subject of the creation of the world; he sneers at anyone whose views are not identical to his.

- The philosophy professor became increasingly *dogmatic* as he grew older and became more firmly convinced of his strange theories.

The opinions or ideas *dogmatically* asserted by a *dogmatic* person are known collectively as *dogma*.

ELITE (i LEET) *n*   the best or most select group
- Alison is a member of bowling's *elite;* she bowls like a champion with both her right hand and her left.
- As captain of the football team, Bobby was part of the high school's *elite*, and he never let you forget it.

This word can also be an adjective:
- The presidential palace was defended by an *elite* corps of soldiers known to be loyal to the president.

To be an *elitist* (i LEET ust) is to be a snob; to be *elitist* (adj.) is to be snobby.

EPHEMERAL (i FEM ur al) *adj*   lasting a very short time

Ephemeral comes from Greek and refers to lasting a single day. The word is generally used more loosely to mean "lasting a short time."
- Youth and flowers are both *ephemeral*. They're gone before you know it.
- Some friendships are *ephemeral*.
- The tread on those used tires will probably turn out to be *ephemeral*.

IMPERATIVE (im PER uh tiv) *adj*   completely necessary; vitally important
- The children couldn't quite accept the idea that cleaning up the playroom was *imperative;* they said they didn't mind wading through the toys strewn on the floor, even if they did occasionally fall down and hurt themselves.

Imperative can also be used as a noun, in which case it means a command, order, or requirement.

- A doctor has a moral *imperative* to help sick people instead of playing golf—unless, of course, it's his day off, or the people aren't very sick.

IMPLICATION (im pluh KAY shun) *n* something implied or suggested; ramification

- When you said I looked healthy, was that really meant as an *implication* that I've put on weight?

- A 100-percent cut in our school budget would have troubling *implications*; I simply don't think the children would receive a good education if they didn't have teachers, books, or a school.

Intimation is a close synonym for *implication*. To *imply* something is to suggest it.

- When Peter's girlfriend said, "My, you certainly know how to drive a car fast, don't you?" in a trembling voice, she was *implying* that Peter was going too fast.

To *imply* something is not at all the same thing as to *infer* (in FUR) it, even though people often use these two words interchangeably. To *infer* is to figure out what is being *implied*. The act of *inferring* is an *inference* (IN fur ens).

- Peter was so proud of his driving that he did not *infer* the meaning of his girlfriend's *implication*.

INSINUATE (in SIN yoo ayt) *v* to hint; to creep in

- When I told her that I hadn't done any laundry in a month, Valerie *insinuated* that I was a slob.

- He didn't ask us outright to leave; he merely *insinuated*, through his tone and his gestures, that it was time for us to go.

- Jessica *insinuated* her way into the conversation by moving her chair closer and closer to where we were sitting.

To *insinuate* is to make an *insinuation*.

MYRIAD (MIR ee ud) *n*   a huge number
- A country sky on a clear night is filled with a *myriad* of stars.
- There are a *myriad* of reasons why I don't like school.

This word can also be used as an adjective.
- *Myriad* stars are a lot of stars.
- The teenager was weighted down by the *myriad* anxieties of adolescence.

PREDILECTION (pred uh LEK shun) *n*   a natural preference for something
- The impatient judge had a *predilection* for well-prepared lawyers who said what they meant and didn't waste his time.
- Joe's *predilection* for saturated fats has added roughly six inches to his waistline in the past ten years.

PROVISIONAL (pruh VIZH uh nul) *adj*   conditional; temporary; tentative
- Louis had been accepted as a *provisional* member of the club. He wouldn't become a permanent member until the other members had had a chance to see what he was really like.
- The old man's offer to donate $10,000 to the charity was *provisional*; he said that he would give the money only if the charity could manage to raise a matching sum.

RAPTURE (RAP chur) *n*   ecstasy; bliss; unequaled joy
- Nothing could equal the American tourists' *rapture* on spotting a popular fast-food restaurant in Calcutta; they had been terrified that they were going to have to eat unfamiliar food.
- Winning an Oscar sent Dustin into a state of *rapture*. "I can't believe this is happening to me!" he exclaimed.

To be full of *rapture* is to be *rapturous* (RAP chur us).
- Omar doesn't go in for *rapturous* expressions of affection; a firm handshake and a quick punch on the shoulder are enough for him.

Rapt is an adjective that refers to being entranced or ecstatic.

- The children listened with *rapt* attention to the storyteller; they didn't notice the pony standing in the hallway behind them.

To be *enraptured* (en RAP churd) is to be enthralled or in a state of *rapture*.

- *Enraptured* by Danielle Steele's thrilling prose style, Frank continued reading until the library was ready to close.

SECT (sekt) *n* a small religious subgroup or religion; any group with a uniting theme or purpose

- Jack dropped out of college and joined a religious *sect* whose members were required to live with animals and surrender all their material possessions to the leaders of the *sect*.

- After the schism of 1949, the religious denomination split into about fifty different *sects*, all of them with near identical beliefs and none of them speaking to the others.

Matters pertaining to *sects* are *sectarian* (sek TER ee un).

- The company was divided by *sectarian* fighting between the research and marketing departments, each of which had its own idea about what the new computer should be able to do.

To be *sectarian* is also to be single-mindedly devoted to a *sect*. *Nonsectarian* means not pertaining to any particular *sect* or group.

- Milly has grown so *sectarian* since becoming a Moonie that she can't really talk to you anymore without trying to convert you.

SECULAR (SEK yuh lur) *adj* having nothing to do with religion or spiritual concerns

- The group home had several nuns on its staff, but it was an entirely *secular* operation; it was run by the city, not the church.

- The priest's *secular* interests include eating German food and playing the trombone.

STAGNATION (stag NAY shun) *n*   motionlessness; inactivity

- The company grew quickly for several years; then it fell into *stagnation.*

- Many years of carelessly dumping garbage next to the river led to the gradual *stagnation* of the water because the trash covered the bottom and made an impromptu dam.

To fall into *stagnation* is to *stagnate.* To be in a state of *stagnation* is to be *stagnant.*

UTILITARIAN (yoo til uh TAR ee un) *adj*   stressing usefulness or utility above all other qualities; pragmatic

- Jason's interior-decorating philosophy was strictly *utilitarian;* if an object wasn't genuinely useful, he didn't want it in his home.

Utilitarian can also be a noun. Jason, just aforementioned, could be called a *utilitarian.*

PART IV

Math Vocabulary

CHAPTER 10

Math Terms for the SAT

SAT Math: The Terms You Need to Know

Vocabulary is not just for the Reading section of the SAT. Math problems, too, require knowing some key terms. Here are the most important terms you will see in math questions on the SAT as well as other standardized tests.

ABSOLUTE VALUE   the distance from zero on the number line, represented by the symbol | |

> **Example:** The absolute value of |–40| is 40.

ARC   any segment of a circle's circumference

AREA   the amount of space within the boundaries of a shape

BISECT   to cut in half

CENTRAL ANGLE   an angle formed by two radii in a circle

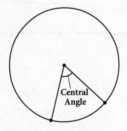

CHORD   any line segment connecting two points on the edge of a circle

CIRCLE   a round figure equaling 360 degrees

CIRCUMFERENCE   the perimeter of (distance around) a circle

CIRCUMSCRIBED   surrounded by another shape that is as small as necessary

COEFFICIENT   a number multiplied by a variable or other algebraic term

> **Example:** In $3x^2$, 3 is the coefficient.

COLLINEAR   referring to points that lie on the same line

COMPLEX NUMBER   a numerical expression that includes an imaginary component (such as i)

COMPOUND INTEREST   In finance, *compound interest* ensures that the amount of interest earned will increase over time.

> **Example:** Sara invests $1,000 in a money market account earning 1% annual interest. The first year she will earn $10 in interest, but the second year she will earn 1% of $1,010. Her interest *compounds* over time.

CONE   A right circular cone (shown below) is the only type you will see on the SAT.

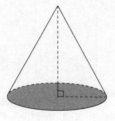

CONGRUENT   equal in size

CONSECUTIVE (NUMBER)   in increasing order

> **Example:** 1, 2, 3, 4, 5... are consecutive numbers.

CONSTANT   a variable whose value is unknown but unchanging

CUBIC FUNCTION in graphing, a representation of an equation in the form $ax^3 + bx^2 + cx + d$

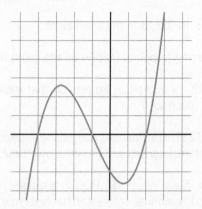

CYLINDER A *right circular cylinder* (shown below) is the only type you will see on the SAT.

DECIMAL a way of expressing a fraction in which numbers are divided by 10, 100, 1,000, and other powers of ten

Example: 2.567 is a decimal.

DIAGONAL in geometry, a line segment connecting opposite vertices of a shape

DIAMETER The distance of a line that connects two points on the edge of a circle, passing through the center. It is the longest line in a circle and equal to twice the radius.

DIFFERENCE   the result of subtraction

> **Example:** The difference between 2 and 5 is 3.

DIGIT   an integer 0 through 9

DIRECT PROPORTION (DIRECT VARIATION)   As one variable increases, so does the other.

> **Example:** It takes Mark 5 hours to bake three-dozen donuts. It takes him 10 hours to bake six-dozen donuts.

DISTINCT   different

> **Example:** 2 and 3 are distinct numbers; 10 and 10 are not distinct.

DIVISIBLE   capable of being evenly divided by another number—that is, with no remainder

> **Example:** 6 is divisible by 2.

EQUATION   a mathematical statement in which one quantity equals another

> **Example:** $x + 3 = y - 2$

EQUILATERAL   a three-sided figure in which all three sides are equal. Each angle equals 60 degrees.

EVEN   divisible by 2

> **Example:** 2, 4, and 6 are even numbers.

EXPONENT/POWER   a number that indicates how many times to multiply a base by itself

> **Example:** $6^3 = 6 \times 6 \times 6$

EXPONENTIAL GROWTH   The increase in one variable occurs at a rate that is exponentially proportionate to another variable, as shown in the graph below.

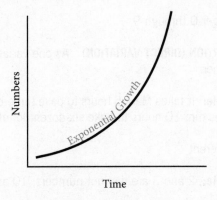

EXPRESSION   a mathematical statement that does not contain an equals sign, which makes it different from an equation

>   **Example:** $x + 3y$

EXTERIOR ANGLE   an angle outside of a figure that is supplementary (allows two angles to equal 180 degrees)

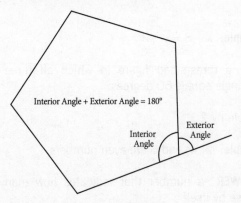

FACTOR   integers that multiply together to make a given product

>   **Example:** 2 and 5 are factors of 10.

FRACTION   a way of expressing the division of numbers by stacking one over the other

Example: $\dfrac{3}{4}$

FUNCTION   a relationship between a set of inputs (*x*-values) and a set of outputs (*y*-values)

Example: $f(x) = 4 - x$

HISTOGRAM   a graphical representation of numerical data; also known as a bar graph

IMAGINARY NUMBER   the square or any other even root of a negative number

INCLUSIVE   including any two endpoints

INDIRECT PROPORTION (INVERSE VARIATION)   a proportion in which one variable increases as another variable decreases, or vice versa

Example: It takes Mrs. Smith 30 minutes to drive to school if she drives at 30 miles per hour. If she drives 60 miles per hour, it takes her only 15 minutes.

INEQUALITY   similar to an equation but always involving a $<$, $>$, $\leq$, or $\geq$ sign

Example: $x < 10$

INSCRIBED (ANGLE IN A CIRCLE)   an angle in a circle with its vertex on the circumference

INTEGER   any real number except decimals or fractions (including 0)

ISOCELES (TRIANGLE)   A triangle in which two sides are equal. The two angles opposite the equal sides are also equal.

LINEAR FUNCTION a function that, when graphed, produces a straight line

>   **Example:** The slope-intercept form of a linear equation is $y = mx + b$.

LINEAR GROWTH a condition in which variables increase at a steady rate, as shown in the graph below

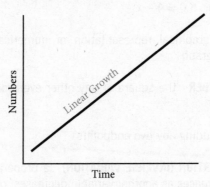

MAXIMUM the highest point, or greatest *y*-value, on a graph of a function

MEAN also known as the *average,* the sum of a list of numbers divided by the quantity of numbers in the list

>   **Example:** The mean of 10 and 20 is 15, since $\dfrac{10 + 20}{2} = 15$.

MEDIAN the middle number in a list of numbers arranged in ascending order, or the average of the two numbers in the middle of the list

>   **Example:** The median of 1, 2, 3, 4, 5 is 3.

MODE   the most frequently occurring number in a list

> **Example:** The mode of 2, 2, 3, 4 is 2.

MINIMUM   the lowest point, or smallest *y*-value, on a graph of a function

MULTIPLE   the product of an integer and another integer

> **Example:** The multiples of 10 are 10, 20, 30, 40, etc.

> Multiples can also be negative (e.g., –10, –20, –30, –40) unless otherwise noted.

NEGATIVE   a number less than 0

ODD   a number not divisible by 2

OF   in word problems, the word that translates to "multiplied by"

> **Example:** What is $\dfrac{2}{3}$ of 60?
>
> $\dfrac{2}{3} \times 60 = 40$

ORDERED PAIR   in the coordinate plane, (*x*, *y*)

ORIGIN   in the coordinate plane, the point (0, 0)

OUTLIER   in statistics, a number that is unusual or deviates strongly from a given list

> **Example:** 10,000 is the outlier in the list 10, 20, 30, 10,000.

PARABOLA   a graph of a quadratic equation, as shown in the graph below

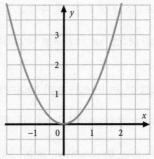

PARALLEL LINES   lines that never intersect

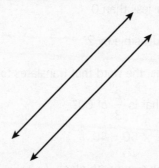

PARALLELOGRAM   A four-sided figure whose
- opposite sides are parallel and equal
- opposite angles are equal
- adjacent angles are supplementary (add up to 180 degrees)
- area = base × height = bh
- height is the perpendicular distance from the base to the opposite side

PER   in word problems, the word that means "divided by"

> **Example:** Angie routinely drives her motorbike at 100 miles per hour.

PERCENT any number divided by 100

> **Example:** 20% means $\dfrac{20}{100}$.

PERPENDICULAR Two lines that form a 90° angle where they meet. The sign for *perpendicular* is ⊥.

PLANE a flat surface extending in all directions

POLYGON In geometry, a shape with multiple sides, usually more than 4. A *regular polygon* has equal sides and angles.

POLYNOMIAL an expression with multiple terms

> **Example:** $x^2 + 2x + 9$

POSITIVE a number greater than 0

PRIME (NUMBER) an integer greater than 1 that is divisible only by 1 and itself

> **Example:** 2, 3, 5, 7, 11, 13, 17, 19...
>
> *Note:* 0 and 1 are not prime numbers.

PROBABILITY $\dfrac{number\ of\ outcomes\ meeting\ a\ requirement}{total\ number\ of\ outcomes}$

> **Example:** When playing a dice game, the probability of rolling a 6 is $\dfrac{1}{6}$.

PRODUCT the result of multiplication

> **Example:** The product of 5 and 7 is 35.

PROFIT in word problems, the amount someone or something makes after costs have been subtracted

> **Example:** If John buys widgets for $100 and sells them for $150, his profit is $50.

QUADRANT one of the four sections of the coordinate plane, numbered as follows:

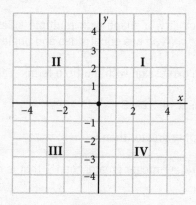

QUADRATIC EQUATION an equation in the form $ax^2 + bx + c = 0$

QUADRILATERAL a four-sided figure

QUOTIENT the result of division

> **Example:** The quotient of 10 divided by 2 is 5.

RADIAN an alternative to measuring angles in degrees

> **Example:** A full circle contains 2π radians.

RADIUS in geometry, a line that extends from the center of the circle to its outer edge, as shown below

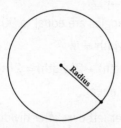

RANGE in statistics, the difference between the largest number and the smallest number in a list

RATE $\dfrac{distance}{time}$

In word problems, *average speed* is simply another way of saying "rate."

RATIO a comparison of "parts" to "parts"

Example: In order to make fruit punch, Debra needs 2 parts orange juice to every 5 parts pineapple juice. The ratio is $\dfrac{2}{5}$, or 0.4.

REAL NUMBER any number that is not imaginary

RECIPROCAL the inverse of a number (when you flip the numerator and denominator)

Example: $\dfrac{2}{3}$ is the reciprocal of $\dfrac{3}{2}$.

RECTANGLE *Rectangles* are special parallelograms; therefore, any fact about parallelograms also applies to rectangles. Rectangles have the following properties:

- Each of the four angles are equal to 90 degrees.

- area = length × width = *lw*

- perimeter = 2(length) + 2(width) = 2*l* + 2*w*

- The diagonals are equal.

REMAINDER the number left over after dividing

> **Example:** When 10 is divided by 8, the remainder is 2.

REVENUE in word problems, a word that means "total money earned"

SCATTERPLOT a set of data represented on a graph by multiple dots, typically forming a linear pattern

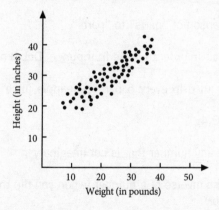

SECTOR Any part of the area formed by two radii and the outside of a circle. The area of a *sector* is proportional to the size of the interior angle.

SIMILAR TRIANGLES triangles that have identical angle measurements and proportionate sides

SLOPE the ratio between the vertical *rise* and the horizontal *run* of a line

$$\text{slope} = \frac{y_2 - y_1}{x_2 - x_1}$$

SOLUTION a known value or set of values

> **Example:** In the equation $x + 5 = 15$, the solution is $x = 10$. Some equations have more than one solution.

SQUARE *Squares* are special rectangles; therefore, any fact about rectangles also applies to squares. Squares have the following properties:

- All four sides are equal.
- area = (side)^2 = s^2
- perimeter = 4(side) = $4s$
- The diagonals are perpendicular.

STANDARD DEVIATION A measure used to quantify how much the data in a set *deviates* from the *standard* (mean). A low standard deviation means that the numbers are close together, while a high standard deviation means that the numbers are spread out over a large range.

SUM the result of addition

> **Example:** The sum of 5 and 6 is 11.

SURFACE AREA the sum of the areas of each face of a three-dimensional figure

SYSTEM OF EQUATIONS two or more equations, generally with two or more variables

> **Example:** $x + 2y = 9$
> $x + 4y = 20$

TANGENT LINE *Tangent* means intersecting at one point. A line tangent to a circle intersects exactly one point on the circumference of the circle. Two circles that touch at only one point are also tangent. A *tangent line* to a circle is always perpendicular to the radius drawn to that point of intersection.

UNDEFINED An equation is *undefined* when it involves the square root of a negative number (imaginary) or dividing by 0.

VARIABLE an unknown quantity, usually represented by a letter such as *x, y, a, b,* etc.

VERTEX In plane geometry, the corners of a shape. For example, a triangle has three vertices. In coordinate geometry, the vertex of a parabola is the "trough" of the graph.

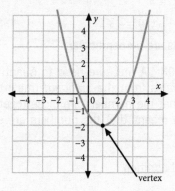

VOLUME the amount of space a three-dimensional object displaces (as in the air or water)

XY-PLANE another name for the coordinate plane; a Cartesian system of two axes: horizontal (*x*) and vertical (*y*)

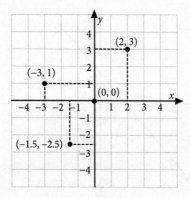

X-INTERCEPT the *x*-coordinate of the point at which a line crosses the *x*-axis

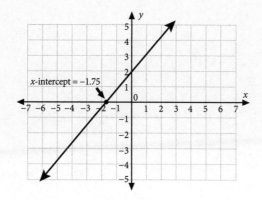

Y-INTERCEPT   the *y*-coordinate of the point at which a line crosses the *y*-axis

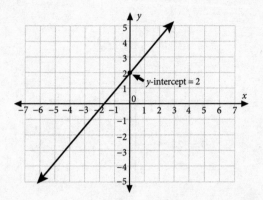

y-intercept = 2

CONCLUSION

Building Your Vocabulary: Strategies and Study Tips

Building a Solid Vocabulary: Long-Term Strategies

You have officially made it through *SAT Power Vocab!* You've learned common Latin and Greek word roots that will help you figure out the meaning of tons of vocabulary words, including those likely to appear on the SAT. You have also learned effective strategies for remembering the meaning of those words, like visual mnemonic devices and word associations. On top of that, you have had the opportunity to put this knowledge to the test with a wide variety of practice exercises, puzzles, and SAT-style quizzes. But now it's time to think about how to take this newfound knowledge *beyond* this book. So, before we leave you, here's some final advice for building your vocabulary for the SAT, the classroom, and your everyday life.

Read, Read, Read

In addition to reading this book, an excellent way to build a solid, sophisticated vocabulary in the long term is to read voraciously. Reading not only brings you into contact with new words, but also forces you to figure out what those new words mean. If you read widely enough, you will find that your vocabulary will build itself. New words are contagious if you give yourself enough exposure to them.

Use a Dictionary

The natural way to learn new vocabulary is by paying attention to how other people use them—that is, to see or hear the word in context. However, while context may give you a clue as to how to use the word, relying on context alone has its pitfalls, which is why we recommend always recommend consulting a dictionary. Here's why.

When you encounter a new word, you can't be certain how to pronounce it unless you hear it spoken by someone whose pronunciation is authoritative. You also can't be sure that the word is being used correctly. Even skillful writers and speakers occasionally misuse language. A writer or speaker may even misuse a word intentionally, perhaps for dramatic or comedic effect.

Even more important, most words have multiple meanings. Sometimes the difference between one meaning and another is slight; sometimes it's enormous. Even if you deduce the meaning from the context, you have no way of knowing whether the meaning you've deduced will apply in other cases.

Finally, context can be misleading, as shown in the example below. The following conversation is a dialogue teachers may find themselves having over and over again with their students. The dialogue concerns the meaning of the word *formidable,* although you can substitute just about any medium-difficult word.

> **Teacher:** Do you know what *formidable* means?
>
> **Student:** Sure, of course.
>
> **Teacher:** Good. Define it.
>
> **Student:** Okay. A formidable opponent is someone...

Here, the student is starting to give an example of how to use the word in a sentence rather than actually defining it, which is a common response to being asked to define a word. Moreover, *formidable* is an interesting case because it is often thought to mean skillful or challenging, as in a *formidable opponent.* The true definition of *formidable,* however, is "causing fear or dread"; it can also mean "awe-inspiring."

The point is that context can be misleading, particularly when you rely exclusively on context to supply you with the meanings of new words. You may hit upon a meaning that seems to fit the context only to discover later that your guess was far wide of the mark. To keep this from happening, use a dictionary.

Define It in Your Own Words
To understand a word completely and make it yours, try to define it in your own words. Don't settle for the dictionary definition. For that matter, don't settle for our definition. Make up your own definition. You'll understand the meaning better. What's more, you'll be more likely to remember it.

Use the Method That Works Best for You

Different study strategies work better for different people. What works for your friend may not work for you, and vice versa. The key is to find an approach that helps you remember the meanings of new words permanently and incorporate them into your everyday vocabulary.

In all likelihood, as you worked through this book you probably had to tailor your approach to fit your own personal learning style. You may have even found that one strategy worked for learning certain words, while an entirely different strategy was better for learning other words. That's all totally fine. Use the one or ones that suit *you* best.

Write It Down

Many people find that they can learn new information more readily if they write it down. The physical act of writing seems to plant the information more firmly in your mind. Perhaps the explanation is that by writing you are bringing another sense into play. (You've seen the word, you've said and heard the word, and now you're *feeling* the word by writing it down.)

You may find it useful to spend some time writing down phrases or sentences incorporating each new word you learn. This is a good way to practice and strengthen your spelling as well.

And don't stop at the word and its definition—also write down any effective mnemonics or mental images you come up with to help you remember it. You may also want to write down the word's etymology, or even draw a picture or diagram.

Put It All Together with Flashcards

A flashcard is a simple piece of paper, usually an index card, with a word on the front of the card and its definition on the back. You may have used flashcards when you were first learning how to read or when you were first tackling a foreign language. Used in the proper spirit, flashcards can turn learning into a game.

SAT Power Vocab

Along with the word's definition, you should also include the pronunciation if you aren't sure you'll remember it. Then you can either practice independently or have a friend quiz you.

Here's a basic flashcard, front and back:

Front

Oblique

Back

(oh-BLEEK)
indirect, at an angle

You'll learn even more if you use your imagination to make the backs of your flashcards a bit more elaborate. For example, you might decorate the back of this card with a diagram of *oblique* lines—that is, lines that are neither parallel nor perpendicular to each other, as shown on the next page.

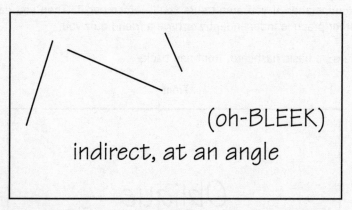

(oh-BLEEK)
indirect, at an angle

Your diagram now provides a mental image that can help you remember the word. You can even use the word itself to create a picture that conveys the meaning of the word and that will stick in your mind to help you remember it.

Here's one possibility. We've divided the word into two parts and written them on two different lines that—surprise!—are at an *oblique* angle to each other:

Back

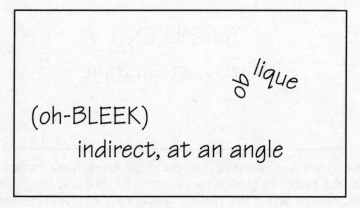

ob lique
(oh-BLEEK)
indirect, at an angle

Practicing with flashcards can be fun. And every time you look at the back of the card, you'll be reminded of the mnemonic, word association, or visual aid you've devised to keep the word firmly in your memory.

Tuck a few flashcards into your pocket before you head out the door in the morning and work on them in spare moments— for instance, while riding on a bus or while listening to the radio. The more often you flash through your flashcards, the faster you'll build your vocabulary.

Be sure to keep track of the words you know and the ones you struggle with so that you can spend more time on the latter group.

Going Beyond This Book

You've worked hard. You've studied every chapter in this book and you now know hundreds of words that you didn't know before. Surely you will encounter some words in the future, though, that you don't know. How do you deal with those? Here, pulling together everything we discussed in this book, is our step-by-step approach to remembering words in the long term and incorporating them into your vocabulary:

Step 1.	Try to deduce the word's meaning from context.
Step 2.	Look it up!
Step 3.	Note the spelling.
Step 4.	Say the word out loud.
Step 5.	Read the main definition. Scan the secondary definitions.
Step 6.	(If you have time) Compare the definition with the definitions and usages of the word's synonyms.
Step 7.	Define the word using your own words.
Step 8.	Use the word in a sentence.
Step 9.	Attach the word to a mnemonic, mental image, or other memory aid.
Step 10.	Make flashcards.
Step 11.	Use the new word every chance you get.

Let's take a look at each of these steps.

Step 1: Try to Deduce the Word's Meaning from Context

As touched on earlier, context will sometimes lead you astray, but doing a bit of detective work is a good way to sharpen your mind and hone your reading comprehension skills. And who knows? You might even guess the right meaning.

Step 2: Look It Up!

Most people try to skip this step. Don't. You won't know whether you're correct about the meaning of a new word until you've consulted a dictionary to check the definition.

Many good dictionaries aren't terribly expensive, but if you don't have one, try an online dictionary or dictionary app.

Step 3: Note the Spelling

Pay attention to how the word is spelled. Then close your eyes and try to reconstruct the spelling in your mind. If you have trouble visualizing the word, test yourself by writing the word on scrap paper and checking your spelling against the dictionary's.

Additionally, compare the spelling variations with other spelling variations you know. This can be an effective trick that helps you recognize words that you think you don't know. For example, *sober* is an adjective; the noun form is *sobriety*. With this as a clue, the noun *propriety* relates to what adjective? *Proper*. *Propriety* refers to what is socially proper or acceptable.

Here's another example: Do you know what *incisive* means? Consider the word *decisive*. *Decisive* relates to the word *decision*. Now, what noun do you think *incisive* relates to? *Incision*. *Incisive* means "sharp" or "cutting," as in an *incisive remark* or an *incisive observation*.

Step 4: Say the Word Out Loud

Say the word *out loud*. Hearing how the word sounds will bring another sense into play and help you remember it.

Step 5: Read the Main Definition; Scan the Secondary Definitions

Most dictionaries list the definitions of multiple-meaning words in order of importance. That does not mean, of course, that the first definition is the one you are looking for. Read *all* of the definitions listed; each will add to and broaden your understanding of the word.

Step 6: Compare the Definition with the Definitions and Usages of the Word's Synonyms

This step takes a little extra time, but believe us when we say that it is time well spent. Again, seeing how a word is similar to or different from synonyms or related words enhances your understanding of all of them.

Step 7: Define the Word Using Your Own Words

We said it before, and we'll say it again: You don't truly know what a word means unless you can define it in your own way. Make the word your own.

Step 8: Use the Word in a Sentence

Now that you know what the word means and can define it in your own terms, use it. Make up a sentence.

It helps to use the word in a sentence that includes a person, thing, or event that you know and that creates a concrete feeling or image. For example, the sentence "They are gregarious" is not as good as "Greg, Gertrude, and Gretchen are gregarious." A more specific sentence will allow you to understand and remember the word.

Step 9: Attach the Word to a Mnemonic, Mental Image, or Other Memory Aid

With all that you've done with the word in the previous steps, you may already have memorized it. The only way to be sure, however, is to connect the word with a mnemonic. You can use our suggestions for the words covered in Part II or come up with your own.

Step 10: Make Flashcards

The paperwork is very important, particularly if you're trying to learn a lot of new words in a short period of time.

Step 11: Use the New Word Every Chance You Get

Dare to be repetitious. Think of your new word knowledge as a muscle that you have to keep working out. If you don't keep new knowledge in shape, you won't keep it at all.

Feel Empowered

We hope that this book will be a valuable resource for you as you continue your SAT prep. Although studying vocabulary for the test is certainly different than it once was, you can prepare by focusing on the areas we've covered here, such as word roots and mnemonics. We also hope that you carry these skills and strategies with you throughout high school, college, and beyond. Words are powerful tools, so understand them and use them well.

Glossary

Glossary

This glossary is divided into two parts. The Master Word List covers *all* of the vocabulary words covered in this book, while the Cram List contains the 50 most important words you absolutely should know before you take the SAT. Study the Cram List first if you're short on prep time before your exam.

Master Word List

ABSTRUSE (ab STROOS) *adj*   hard to understand

ACQUISITIVE (uh KWIZ uh tiv) *adj*   seeking or tending to acquire; greedy

ACUTE (uh KYOOT) *adj*   sharp; shrewd; discerning

ADVOCATE (AD vuh kut)
- *n*   a person who argues in favor of a position or cause
- *v*   to argue in favor of a position or cause

AFFRONT (uh FRUNT) *n*   an insult; a deliberate act of disrespect

ALLEVIATE (uh LEE vee ayt) *v*   to relieve, usually temporarily or incompletely; to make bearable; to lessen

ALLOCATE (AL uh kayt) *v*   to distribute; to assign; to allot

AMBIGUOUS (am BIG yoo us) *adj*   unclear in meaning; confusing; capable of being interpreted in different ways

AMBIVALENT (am BIV uh lunt) *adj*   undecided; having opposing feelings simultaneously

AMENABLE (uh MEE nuh bul *or* uh MEH nuh bul) *adj*   obedient; willing to give in to the wishes of another; agreeable

AMIABLE (AY mee uh bul) *adj*   friendly; agreeable

AMORAL (ay MOR ul) *adj* lacking a sense of right and wrong; neither good nor bad, neither moral nor immoral; without moral feelings

AMOROUS (AM ur us) *adj* feeling loving, especially in a romantic sense; in love; relating to love

AMORPHOUS (uh MOR fus) *adj* shapeless; without a regular or stable shape; blob-like

ANACHRONISM (uh NAK ruh niz um) *n* something out of place in time or history; an incongruity

ANALOGY (uh NAL uh jee) *n* a comparison of one thing to another; similarity

ANECDOTE (AN ik doht) *n* a short account of a humorous or revealing incident; a story

ANNEX (uh NEKS) *v* to add or attach

ANOMALY (uh NAHM uh lee) *n* an unusual occurrence; an irregularity; a deviation

ANTHOLOGY (an THAHL uh jee) *n* a collection, especially of literary works

ANTHROPOMORPHIC (an thruh puh MOHR fik) *adj* ascribing human characteristics to nonhuman animals or objects

ANTIPATHY (an TIP uh thee) *n* firm dislike; a dislike

ANTIPODAL (an TIP ud ul) *adj* situated on opposite sides of the Earth; exactly opposite

ANTITHESIS (an TITH uh sis) *n* the direct opposite

APATHY (AP uh thee) *n* lack of interest; lack of feeling

APPREHENSIVE (ap ruh HEN siv) *adj* worried; anxious

ASCERTAIN (as ur TAYN) *v* to determine with certainty; to find out definitely

ASSIMILATE (uh SIM uh layt) *v* to take in; to absorb; to learn thoroughly

ASTUTE (uh STOOT) *adj* shrewd; keen in judgment

ASYLUM (uh SYE lum) *n* refuge; a place of safety

AUTOCRATIC (aw tuh KRAT ik) *adj* ruling with absolute authority; extremely bossy

AUTONOMOUS (aw TAHN uh mus) *adj* acting independently

BENEDICTION (ben uh DIK shun) *n* a blessing; an utterance of good wishes

BENEFACTOR (BEN uh fak tur) *n* one who provides help, especially in the form of a gift or donation

BENEVOLENT (beh NEV uh lunt) *adj* generous; kind; doing good deeds

BENIGN (bih NYNE) *adj* gentle; not harmful; kind; mild

BLUSTER (BLUS tur) *v* to roar; to be loud; to be tumultuous

BOMBAST (BAHM bast) *n* pompous or pretentious speech or writing

BRAWN (brawn) *n* big muscles; great strength

BREVITY (BREV i tee) *n* the quality or state of being brief in duration

BURGEON (BUR jun) *v* to expand; to flourish

CALLOUS (KAL us) *adj* insensitive; emotionally hardened

CANDOR (KAN dur) *n* truthfulness; sincere honesty

CASTIGATE (KAS tuh gayt) *v* to criticize severely; to chastise

CEREBRAL (suh REE brul) *adj* brainy; intellectually refined

CHRONIC (KRAHN ik) *adj* occurring often and repeatedly over a period of time; lasting a long time; inveterate

CHRONICLE (KRAHN uh kul) *n* a record of events in order of time; a history

CIRCUMNAVIGATE (sur kum NAV uh gayt) *v* to sail or travel all the way around

CIRCUMSCRIBE (SUR kum skrybe) *v* to draw a line around; to set the limits; to define; to restrict

CIRCUMSPECT (SUR kum spekt) *adj* cautious

CIRCUMVENT (sur kum VENT) *v* to get around something in a clever, occasionally dishonest way

COMPLACENT (kum PLAY sunt) *adj* self-satisfied; overly pleased with oneself; contented to a fault

CONGREGATE (KAHN grih gayt) *v* to come together

CONSPICUOUS (kun SPIK yoo us) *adj* easily seen; impossible to miss

CONTIGUOUS (kun TIG yoo us) *adj* side by side; adjoining

CONTRABAND (KAHN truh band) *n* smuggled goods

CONTRETEMPS (KAHN truh tahn) *n* an embarrassing occurrence; a mishap

CORRUGATED (KOHR uh gay tud) *adj* shaped with folds or waves

COSMOPOLITAN (kahz muh PAHL uh tun) *adj* at home in many places or situations; internationally sophisticated

CREDULOUS (KREJ uh lus) *adj*   eager to believe; gullible

CULPABLE (KUL puh bul) *adj*   deserving blame; guilty

DEBASE (di BAYS) *v*   to lower in quality or value; to degrade

DEBILITATE (di BIL uh tayt) *v*   to weaken; to cripple

DEBUNK (di BUNK) *v*   to expose the nonsense of

DECRY (di KRY) *v*   to put down; to denounce

DEFAME (di FAYM) *v*   to libel or slander; to ruin the good name of

DEFERENCE (DEF ur uns) *n*   submission to another's will; respect; courtesy

DEFILE (di FYLE) *v*   to make filthy or foul; to desecrate

DEFUNCT (di FUNKT) *adj*   no longer in effect; no longer in existence

DEGENERATE (di JEN uh rayt) *v*   to break down; to deteriorate

DEGRADE (di GRAYD) *v*   to lower in dignity or status; to corrupt; to deteriorate

DEIGN (dayn) *v*   to condescend; to think it in accordance with one's dignity (to do something)

DEJECTED (di JEK tid) *adj*   depressed; disheartened

DENOMINATION (di nahm uh NAY shun) *n*   a classification; a category name

DENOUNCE (di NOWNS) *v*   to condemn openly

DEPLETE (di PLEET) *v*   to decrease the supply of; to exhaust; to use up

DEPLORE (di PLOHR) *v*   to regret; to condemn; to lament

DERIDE (di RYDE) *v* to ridicule; to laugh at contemptuously

DESPONDENT (dih SPAHN dunt) *adj* extremely depressed; full of despair

DEXTROUS (DEX trus) *adj* skillful; adroit

DICTUM (DIK tum) *n* an authoritative saying; an adage; a maxim; a proverb

DISDAIN (DIS dayn) *v* to regard with contempt (This word can also be an adjective.)

DISPARAGE (dih SPAR ij) *v* to belittle; to say uncomplimentary things about, usually in a somewhat indirect way

DISPARATE (DIS pur it) *adj* different; incompatible; unequal

DISTINGUISH (di STING gwish) *v* to tell apart; to cause to stand out

DOGMATIC (dawg MAT ik) *adj* arrogantly assertive of unproven ideas; stubbornly claiming that something (often a system of beliefs) is beyond dispute

DUBIOUS (DOO bee us) *adj* full of doubt; uncertain

ELITE (i LEET) *n* the best or most select group

ELOCUTION (el uh KYOO shun) *n* the art of public speaking (A related word is *eloquent,* which means "well-spoken.")

ELUSIVE (ih LOO siv) *adj* hard to pin down; evasive

EMPATHY (EM puh thee) *n* identification with the feelings or thoughts of another

EMPIRICAL (em PIR uh kul) *adj* relying on experience or observation; not merely theoretical

ENCROACH (en KROHCH) *v* to make gradual or stealthy inroads into; to trespass

EPHEMERAL (i FEM ur al) *adj*   lasting a very short time

EPITOME (i PIT uh mee) *n*   a brief summary that captures the meaning of the whole; the perfect example of something; a paradigm

EQUANIMITY (ek wuh NIM uh tee) *n*   composure; calm

EQUITABLE (EK wuh tuh bul) *adj*   fair

EQUIVOCAL (ih KWIV uh kul) *adj*   ambiguous; intentionally confusing; capable of being interpreted in more than one way

ERUDITION (ER eh di shen) *n*   impressive or extensive knowledge, usually achieved by studying and schooling; scholarly knowledge

EULOGY (YOO luh jee) *n*   a spoken or written tribute to a person, especially a person who has just died

EVOKE (i VOHK) *v*   to summon forth; to draw forth; to awaken; to produce or suggest

EXONERATE (ig ZAHN uh rayt) *v*   to free completely from blame; to exculpate

EXORBITANT (ig ZOHR buh tent) *adj*   excessively costly; excessive

EXPATRIATE (eks PAY tree ayt) *v*   to throw (someone) out of his or her native land; to move away from one's native land; to emigrate

EXPEDIENT (ik SPEE dee ent) *adj*   providing an immediate advantage; serving one's immediate self-interest; practical

EXPEDITE (EK spi dyte) *v*   to speed up or ease the progress of

EXPLICIT (ik SPLIS it) *adj*   clearly and directly expressed

FALLACY (FAL uh see) *n*   a false notion or belief; a misconception

FISCAL (FIS kul) *adj*   pertaining to financial matters; monetary

FLAGRANT (FLAY grunt) *adj*   glaringly bad; notorious; scandalous

FLAUNT (flawnt) *v*   to show off; to display ostentatiously

FLEDGLING (FLEJ ling) *adj*   inexperienced or immature

FLIPPANT (FLIP unt) *adj*   frivolously disrespectful; saucy; pert; flip

GAFFE (gaf) *n*   a social blunder; an embarrassing mistake; a faux pas

GREGARIOUS (gruh GAR ee us) *adj*   sociable; enjoying the company of others

IGNOMINY (IG nuh min ee) *n*   deep disgrace

IMPEDE (im PEED) *v*   to obstruct or interfere with; to delay

IMPERATIVE (im PER uh tiv) *adj*   completely necessary; vitally important

IMPLICATION (im pluh KAY shun) *n*   something implied or suggested; ramification (A related word is *implicit,* which means "implied.")

IMPUGN (im PYOON) *v*   to attack, especially to attack the truth or integrity of something

IMPUNITY (im PYOO nuh tee) *n*   freedom from punishment or harm

INDICT (in DYTE) *v*   to charge with a crime; to accuse of wrongdoing

INDIFFERENT (in DIF ur unt) *adj*   not caring one way or the other; apathetic; mediocre

INDIGNANT (in DIG nunt) *adj*   angry, especially as a result of something unjust or unworthy; insulted (The noun form of this word is *indignation.*)

INDOLENT (IN duh lent) *adj*   lazy

INEPT (in EPT) *adj*   clumsy; incompetent

INSINUATE (in SIN yoo ayt) *v*   to hint; to creep in

INSOLENT (IN suh lent) *adj*   arrogant; insulting

INSULAR (IN suh lur) *adj*   like an island; isolated

INTRACTABLE (in TRAK tuh bul) *adj*   uncontrollable; stubborn; disobedient

INVOKE (in VOHK) *v*   to entreat or pray for; to call on as in prayer; to declare to be in effect

IRREVOCABLE (i REV uh kuh bul) *adj*   irreversible

LAMENT (luh MENT) *v*   to mourn

LAUD (lawd) *v*   to praise; to applaud; to extol; to celebrate

LAVISH (LAV ish) *v*   to spend freely or bestow generously; to squander

LUCID (LOO sid) *adj*   clear; easy to understand

LUMINOUS (LOO muh nus) *adj*   giving off light; glowing; bright

MAGNANIMOUS (mag NAN uh mus) *adj*   forgiving; not resentful; noble in spirit; generous

MAGNATE (MAG nayt) *n*   a rich, powerful, or very successful businessperson

MALAISE (ma LAYZ) *n*   a feeling of depression, uneasiness, or queasiness

MALAPROPISM (MAL uh prahp iz um) *n*   humorous misuse of a word that sounds similar to the word intended but has a ludicrously different meaning

MALFEASANCE (mal FEE zuns) *n*   an illegal act, especially by a public official

MALICIOUS (muh LISH us) *adj*   deliberately harmful

MALIGNANT (muh LIG nuhnt) *adj*   causing harm

MALINGER (muh LING ger) *v* to pretend to be sick to avoid doing work

MALLEABLE (MAL ee uh bul) *adj* easy to shape or bend

MEDIATE (MEE dee ayt) *v* to help settle differences (The noun form of this word is *mediation*.)

MERCENARY (MUR suh ner ee) *n* a hired soldier; someone who will do anything for money

MERCURIAL (mur KYOOR ee ul) *adj* emotionally unpredictable; rapidly changing in mood

METAMORPHOSIS (met uh MOR fuh sis) *n* a magical change in form; a striking or sudden change

MISANTHROPIC (mis un THRAHP ik) *adj* hating mankind

MYRIAD (MIR ee ud) *n* a huge number

NEOLOGISM (nee OL uh jiz um) *n* a new word or phrase; a new usage of a word

NIHILISM (NYE uh liz um) *n* the belief that there are no values or morals in the universe

NOMENCLATURE (NOH mun klay chur) *n* a set or system of names; a designation; a terminology

NOMINAL (NOM uh nul) *adj* in name only; insignificant; "A-OK" (during rocket launches)

NOSTALGIA (nahs TAL juh) *n* sentimental longing for the past; homesickness

NOVEL (NAHV ul) *adj* fresh; original; new

OBJECTIVE (ahb JEK tiv) *adj* unbiased; unprejudiced

OBSCURE (ub SKYOOR) *adj* unknown; hard to understand; dark

OMINOUS (AHM uh nus) *adj* threatening; menacing; portending doom

OMNISCIENT (ahm NISH unt) *adj* all-knowing; having infinite wisdom

OPAQUE (oh PAYK) *adj* impossible to see through; impossible to understand

ORTHODOX (OR thuh dahks) *adj* conventional; adhering to established principles or doctrines, especially in religion; by the book

OSCILLATE (AHS uh layt) *v* to swing back and forth; to pulsate; to waver or vacillate between beliefs or ideas

PALLIATE (PAL ee ayt) *v* to relieve or alleviate something without getting rid of the problem; to assuage; to mitigate

PARTISAN (PAHR tuh zun) *n* one who supports a particular person, cause, or idea

PATHOLOGY (puh THAHL uh jee) *n* the science of diseases

PATHOS (PA thos) *n* that which makes people feel pity or sorrow

PEDANTIC (puh DAN tik) *adj* boringly scholarly or academic

PENCHANT (PEN chunt) *n* a strong taste or liking for something; a predilection

PENITENT (PEN uh tunt) *adj* sorry; repentant; contrite

PERIPATETIC (per uh peh TET ik) *adj* wandering; traveling continually; itinerant

PERIPHERY (puh RIF uh ree) *n* the outside edge of something

PERVADE (pur VAYD) *v* to spread throughout

PHILANTHROPY (fi LAN thruh pee) *n* love of mankind, especially by doing good deeds

PLACATE (PLAY kayt) *v*   to pacify; to appease; to soothe

PLACEBO (pluh SEE boh) *n*   a fake medication; a fake medication used as a control in tests of the effectiveness of drugs

POSTERITY (pahs TER uh tee) *n*   future generations; descendants; heirs

POSTHUMOUS (PAHS chuh mus) *adj*   occurring after one's death; published after the death of the author

PRAGMATIC (prag MAT ik) *adj*   practical; down-to-earth; based on experience rather than theory

PREDILECTION (pred uh LEK shun) *n*   a natural preference for something

PRESAGE (PRES ij) *v*   to portend; to foreshadow; to forecast or predict

PROLIFERATE (proh LIF uh rayt) *v*   to spread or grow rapidly

PROLIFIC (proh LIF ik) *adj*   abundantly productive; fruitful or fertile

PROVISIONAL (pruh VIZH uh nul) *adj*   conditional; temporary; tentative

PROVOKE (pruh VOHK) *v*   to cause; to incite; to stir up, especially a feeling or action (The adjective form of this word is *provocative*.)

PRUDENT (PROOD unt) *adj*   careful; having foresight

PSEUDONYM (SOO duh nim) *n*   a false name; an alias

RAPTURE (RAP chur) *n*   ecstasy; bliss; unequaled joy

RECIPROCAL (ri SIP ruh kul) *adj*   mutual; shared; interchangeable (The verb form of this word is *reciprocate*.)

REDUNDANT (ri DUN dunt) *adj*   unnecessarily repetitive; excessive; excessively wordy

REPLETE (ri PLEET) *adj* completely filled; abounding

REPUGNANT (ri PUG nunt) *adj* repulsive; offensive; disgusting

RESIGNATION (rez ig NAY shun) *n* passive submission; acquiescence

RETICENT (RET uh sint) *adj* quiet; restrained; reluctant to speak, especially about oneself

RHETORIC (RET ur ik) *n* the art of formal speaking or writing; inflated discourse

RUDIMENTARY (roo duh MEN tuh ree) *adj* basic; crude; unformed or undeveloped

SAGACIOUS (suh GAY shus) *adj* discerning; shrewd; keen in judgment; wise

SECT (sekt) *n* a small religious subgroup or religion; any group with a uniting theme or purpose

SECULAR (SEK yuh lur) *adj* having nothing to do with religion or spiritual concerns

SOPHOMORIC (sahf uh MOHR ik) *adj* juvenile; childishly goofy

SPECIOUS (SPEE shus) *adj* deceptively plausible or attractive

SQUANDER (SKWAHN dur) *v* to waste

STAGNATION (stag NAY shun) *n* motionlessness; inactivity

SUBSTANTIATE (sub STAN shee ayt) *v* to prove; to verify; to confirm

SUPERFICIAL (soo pur FISH ul) *adj* on the surface only; shallow; not thorough

TANGENTIAL (tan JEN shul) *adj* only superficially related to the matter at hand; not especially relevant; peripheral

TEMPORAL (TEM pur ul) *adj*　pertaining to time; pertaining to life or earthly existence; non-eternal; short-lived

TEMPORIZE (TEM puh ryze) *v*　to stall; to cause delay through indecision

TENTATIVE (TEN tuh tiv) *adj*　experimental; temporary; uncertain

TENUOUS (TEN yoo us) *adj*　flimsy; extremely thin

THWART (thwort) *v*　to prevent from being accomplished; to frustrate; to hinder

UNDERMINE (UN dur myne) *v*　to impair; to subvert; to weaken by excavating underneath

UNDERSCORE (un dur SKOHR) *v*　to underline; to emphasize

VERACITY (vuh RAS uh tee) *n*　truthfulness

VERISIMILITUDE (ver uh si MIL uh tood) *n*　similarity to reality; the appearance of truth; looking like the real thing

VERITY (VER uh tee) *n*　the quality of being true; something true

VESTIGE (VES tij) *n*　a remaining bit of something; a last trace

VEX (veks) *v*　to annoy; to pester; to confuse

VIE (vye) *v*　to compete; to contest; to struggle

VIGILANT (VIJ uh lunt) *adj*　constantly alert; watchful; wary

VOCATION (voh KAY shun) *n*　an occupation; a job

VOCIFEROUS (voh SIF ur us) *adj*　loud; noisy; expressed in a forceful or loud way

VOLITION (voh LISH un) *n*　will; conscious choice

Cram List

ACUTE   sharp; shrewd; discerning
- His hearing was unusually *acute.*

ADVOCATE   *v* to argue in favor of a position or cause; *n* one who argues in favor of a position or cause
- Mr. Smith is a major *advocate* for various environmental causes.

ALLEVIATE   to relieve, usually temporarily or incompletely; to make bearable; to lessen
- Aspirin *alleviates* the pain of a headache.

AMBIVALENT   undecided; having opposing feelings simultaneously
- Amy felt *ambivalent* about her dance class: On the one hand, she enjoyed the exercise; but on the other, the choice of dances bored her.

ANALOGY   a comparison of one thing to another; similarity
- Early internet developers created an *analogy* between viral infections and the popularity of video clips.

ANECDOTE   a short account of an interesting incident
- Uncle Richard is known for his many stories and childhood *anecdotes.*

ANOMALY   an unusual occurrence; an irregularity; a deviation
- James is an *anomaly*; he is equally skilled in both art and science.

APPREHENSIVE   worried; anxious
- My grandmother was very *apprehensive* before her hernia surgery.

ASCERTAIN   to determine with certainty; to find out definitely
- We tried to *ascertain* why the traffic on the highway was backed up for 20 miles.

BENEVOLENT   generous; kind; doing good deeds
- She belonged to many *benevolent* organizations dedicated to helping underprivileged students.

BREVITY   the quality or state of being brief in duration
- Brevity = briefness. (You can't get any shorter than that!)

CANDOR   truthfulness; sincere honesty
- Candace's *candor* overwhelmed her business colleagues, who were not used to such honesty.

COMPLACENT   self-satisfied; overly pleased with oneself; contented to a fault
- Voter turnout is chronically low in this city; many residents are *complacent* about the current state of politics.

CONSPICUOUS   easily seen; impossible to miss
- The red tuxedo was *conspicuous* among all the classic black ones. What was he thinking?
- The antonym of *conspicuous* is *inconspicuous*.

DEBILITATE   to weaken; to cripple
- After contracting the flu, Max was utterly *debilitated*.

DEFERENCE   submission to another's will; respect; courtesy
- The children were taught to show *deference* to their parents.

DENOUNCE   to condemn openly
- In many powerful speeches throughout his lifetime, Martin Luther King, Jr. *denounced* racism as immoral.

DESPONDENT   extremely depressed; full of despair
- The *despondent* supporters of the defeated candidate gasped when he announced that he would suspend his campaign indefinitely.

DISDAIN   to regard with contempt
- The critics *disdained* the new author for his lack of skill.

DISPARAGE to belittle; to say uncomplimentary things about, usually in a somewhat indirect way
- Wanda *disparaged* Glen by calling him a cheat and a liar.

DISTINGUISH to tell apart; to cause to stand out
- We could barely *distinguish* between Mary Kate and Ashley Olsen.

DUBIOUS full of doubt; uncertain
- Jerry's *dubious* claim that he could fly like Superman didn't win him any summer job offers.

ELOQUENT well-spoken
- The speaker was so *eloquent* that we wished we could have heard the speech again.

EMPIRICAL relying on experience or observation; not merely theoretical
- The young medical researcher was sincerely hoping for *empirical* results that would support his hypothesis.

ENCROACH to make gradual or stealthy inroads into; to trespass
- When hiking in the woods, it is best not to *encroach* upon the territory of brown bears.

EVOKE to summon forth; to draw forth; to awaken; to produce or suggest
- His suspicious behavior at the airport *evoked* mistrust in the security guards.

EXPLICIT clearly and directly expressed
- You do not have permission to stay at your friend's house without your mother's *explicit* approval.

IMPERATIVE completely necessary; vitally important
- It is *imperative* to study your vocabulary words!

IMPLICIT implied
- Mark and his mother had an *implicit* agreement not to discuss his failures at work.

INDIFFERENT   not caring one way or the other; apathetic; mediocre
- We should never be *indifferent* to the suffering of others.

INDIGNATION   anger aroused by something perceived as unjust
- The presidential candidate won by expressing *indignation* about the failing economy.

INNOVATION   the act of introducing something new
- The computer industry has succeeded by implementing a series of successful *innovations.*

LAMENT   to mourn
- Jessica *lamented* the death of her grandfather.

MALICIOUS   deliberately harmful
- We tried not to listen to the *malicious* gossip being spread about the new science teacher.

MALLEABLE   easy to shape or bend
- Aluminum is a *malleable* metal appropriate for many industrial uses.

MEDIATION   a settlement between conflicting parties
- John's father is a lawyer who specializes in the *mediation* of labor-management disputes.

NOSTALGIA   sentimental longing for the past; homesickness
- Katrina was often *nostalgic* for her hometown in rural Kansas.

NOVEL   *adj*   fresh; original; new
- It was a *novel* idea, the sort of thing no one had tried before.

OBSCURE   *adj*   unknown; hard to understand; dark
- Some say that James Joyce's writing style is obscure and complex.

OBJECTIVE   *adj*   unbiased; prejudiced;   *n*   a goal
- Judges are expected to make *objective* decisions unaffected by their personal biases.
- It is not our *objective* to win the game; we simply want to have fun.

OMINOUS   menacing; threatening; portending doom
- The tornado was preceded by *ominous* black clouds for as far as the eye could see.

PERVADE   to be present throughout
- The sweet scent of lilacs *pervaded* the garden.

PROVOCATIVE   giving rise to action or feeling
- The senator's *provocative* comments sparked an uproar among even his staunchest supporters.

PRUDENT   careful; having foresight
- Dan became a millionaire after a lifetime of *prudent* investments.

RECIPROCATE   to mutually take or give; to respond in kind
- The chef *reciprocated* his rival's respect; they admired each other so much that they even traded recipes.

RESIGNATION   passive submission; acquiescence
- Tim shrugged with *resignation* after losing his third tennis match in one week.

SUBSTANTIATE   to prove; to verify; to confirm
- The argument was *substantiated* by clear facts and hard evidence.

SUPERFICIAL   on the surface only; shallow; not thorough
- Despite the hype surrounding the second edition of the book, it contained only *superficial* changes.

UNDERMINE   to impair; to subvert; to weaken by excavating underneath
- A lack of sleep can *undermine* one's health and happiness.

UNDERSCORE   to underline; to emphasize
- The rising price of fuel *underscored* the need for greater efficiencies.

Notes

Notes

Notes

Notes

Notes

Notes